thegoodwebguide

world religions

www.thegoodwebguide.co.uk

thegoodwebguide

world religions

Dr Gary Bunt

The Good Web Guide Limited • London

First Published in Great Britain in 2001 by The Good Web Guide Limited
Broadwall House, 21 Broadwall, London, SE1 9PL

www.thegoodwebguide.co.uk

Email: feedback@thegoodwebguide.co.uk

10 9 8 7 6 5 4 3 2 1

A catalogue record for this book is available from the British Library.

ISBN 1-903282-25-X

Project Editor Michelle Clare

Design by Myriad Creative Ltd

Printed in Italy at LEGO S.p.A.

user key

£	Subscription	FR	France	RUS	Russia
R	Registration	GR	Greece	SP	Spain
🔒	Secure	HAI	Haiti	SWI	Switzerland

countries

		IND	India	TIB	Tibet
AUS	Australia	INT	International	UAE	United Arab Emirates
CAN	Canada	IT	Italy	UK	United Kingdom
CUB	Cuba	JAP	Japan	US	United States
DEN	Denmark	NIG	Nigeria		
EGY	Egypt	NL	Netherlands		
FIN	Finland	QAT	Qatar	18	Adults Only

contents

the good web guides

The World Wide Web is a vast resource, with millions of sites on every conceivable subject. There are people who have made it their mission to surf the net: cyber-communities have grown, and people have formed relationships and even married on the net.

However, the reality for most people is that they don't have the time or inclination to surf the net for hours on end. Busy people want to use the internet for quick access to information. You don't have to spend hours on the internet looking for answers to your questions and you don't have to be an accomplished net surfer or cyber wizard to get the most out of the web. It can be a quick and useful resource if you are looking for specific information. The Good Web Guides have been published with this in mind. To give you a head start in your search, our researchers have looked at hundreds of sites and what you will find in the Good Web Guides is a collection of reviews of the best we've found.

The Good Web Guide recommendation is impartial and all of the featured sites have been visited several times. Reviews are focused on the website and what it sets out to do, rather than an endorsement of a company or their product. A small but beautiful site run by a one-man band may be rated higher than an ambitious but flawed site run by a mighty organisation. Relevance to the UK-based visitor is also given a high premium: tantalising as it is to read about purchases you can make in California, because of delivery charges, import duties and controls it may not be as useful as a local site.

Our reviewers considered a number of questions when reviewing the sites, such as: How quickly do the sites and individual pages download? Can you move around the site easily and get back to where you started, and do the links work? Is the information up to date and accurate? And is the site pleasing to the eye and easy to read? More importantly, we also asked whether the site has something distinctive to offer, whether it be entertainment, inspiration or pure information. On the basis of the answers to these questions sites are given ratings out of five. As we aim only to include sites that we feel are of serious interest, there are very few low-rated sites.

Bear in mind that the reviews you see here are just snapshots of the sites at a particular time. The process of choosing and writing about sites is rather like painting the Forth Bridge: as each section appears complete, new sites are launched and others are modified. When you've registered at the Good Web Guide site you can check out the reviews of new sites and updates of existing ones, or even have them emailed to you. By registering at our site, you'll find hot links to all the sites listed, so you can just click and go without needing to type the addresses accurately into your browser.

All our sites have been reviewed by the author and research team, but we'd like to know what you think. Contact us via the website or email feedback@thegoodwebguide.co.uk. You are welcome to recommend sites, quibble about the ratings, point out changes and inaccuracies or suggest new features to assess.

You can find us at www.thegoodwebguide.co.uk

introduction

The Good Web Guide to World Religions rates sites on criteria such as navigability, clarity, download time, and interesting content. The Guide does not set out to establish which religion or tradition is superior to another, rather to provide a snapshot of how world religions are characterised in their many forms on the net today. Major beliefs are well represented in this book, which also gives an entry point to read about other worldviews, ranging from alternative or new religious movements through to individuals who have established their own religions online. A highly rated site about a religion is not necessarily one that has been created by a major organisation, and you will find some accessible and interesting pages that are individual expressions of belief. Conversely, there are some official sites that have not been designed with optimum design or content qualities in mind, lacking clarity and being difficult to navigate. Important web content is often lost because it can be difficult to access or locate, hidden in the dark recesses of cyberspace: in some of the reviews contained in the book, I have tried to unpick the combinations required to find significant materials about religion on the web.

Some readers might be surprised by just how much material about religions is available through the World Wide Web. Ever since the internet first appeared, there have been digital resources associated with various worldviews. With the development of user-friendly browsers and web authoring tools, the amount of online content about world religions has increased considerably, becoming more specialist and interactive in nature. The impact of web pages, email and chatrooms on religious dialogue, expression and development is significant, in areas where there are high net-access levels. Through the internet, there

are new opportunities for the discussion and dissemination of religious ideas. Religion is not dominating the medium in the same way as commerce, pornography, news and sport, but there is a significant amount of religion-related content available. Many of the sites reviewed in this book generate hundreds of thousands of hits (visits) in a year.

Throughout the book, readers will find reviews of unique web resources associated with religion. These include opportunities for 'encounters' with sacred individuals (including deities, prophets, and saints), and 'experiences' of sacred places usually accessible only to devotees. Readers can discover the histories of religions, view unique media materials, and search sacred digital texts. There are even places of contemplation, advice and prayer which can be accessed through the net. The Guide points the way to free resources available online, such as religious music (from cantors to heavy metal) and books (from the Bible to Kama Sutra).

Different, and often competing, websites may represent world religions. The global natures of some belief systems lend themselves to the internet, and many sites have a multi-national and multi-cultural flavour to them. Local sites often mirror the content and doctrines of their central site, a factor that I have attempted to indicate in this guide. There are fascinating individual expressions of belief as well, indicating that globalisation and homogeneity has not impacted on every worldview or belief system. Notions of religious pluralism can be difficult to label, particularly if diverse practices, rituals and sub-traditions fall under the single label of a particular religion. There can also be mystery in religion, and that element of the transcendent finds expression (when tangible) through the sites reviewed in this book. Religion can be a profound and emotional experience for an individual believer; some of this experiential understanding and wisdom is conveyed within sites reviewed in the Guide, which may express a contemplative quest or a unique and expressive dimension to religious life.

Many websites attempt to describe aspects of a sacred text, deity or prophet through a multi-media net interface. This may be articulated and (hyper-) linked to a specific history or doctrine, and/or to prescriptive elements of faith that seek to control or influence societies and individuals in the name of religion. The impact of religion on societies is one dimension of beliefs that can be measured through the internet, which offers many perspectives and opinions, many of them updated regularly in the light of contemporary issues. Experiential information and dialogue that never finds its way into other forms of media has a ready expression on the net, allowing insight and discussion with individuals and organisations beyond more traditional levels of communication. The levels of interactivity can take the web user into new areas of knowledge about their own or other peoples' beliefs, where unmediated 'grass-roots' perspectives can be studied.

The question of balance and reliability of information is important when discussing religions on the internet. A website may not necessarily be as reliable, objective or authoritative as a textbook, however these terms may be defined, and will not always have gone through an editorial process which checks information and other content. The idea that anyone with the appropriate computer and internet access can publish their thoughts and opinions about religion onto the web may be seen as liberating, although it is one thing to publish, and another to be read!

In some contexts, access to equipment is limited, and there may be censorship. There are many fine, individually authored websites (some of which are reviewed in this Guide), but there is also a substantial amount of material that is inadequate, inaccurate, plagiarised, and of generally poor quality. This Guide is an attempt to steer the reader, at least in terms of the quality of websites.

This book does not set out to list every church, mosque, temple, synagogue or shrine which happens to have a website, and neither does it make any claims to being an Encyclopedia of World Religions on the internet; that would require several extensive volumes. What the Guide does do is indicate how to access many religions through the internet, either directly or through the carefully chosen portals. If a particular belief is not included in this Guide, it should be easy to access in its online manifestation (if available) through the entry points that are included. Detailed histories or theologies of particular beliefs are not included in the Guide, as much of this information (from various perspectives) can be obtained through the sites reviewed in the book.

Within the sites listed in this book, there may inevitably be a percentage of polemical 'anti-belief' content, dedicated to criticising or attacking other worldviews. Where possible, I have chosen not to focus on such material because, while it might be interesting, it may not always constitute balanced information about a religion. Inevitably, with a subject such as world religions, some of the sites listed in this Guide may conflict with individual worldviews or be seen as controversial by some readers. I hope, however, that their presence helps contribute to the reader's awareness of religion on the internet, even if particular readers don't agree with a site's content or inclusion.

The selection of sites became problematic when we were dealing with religious perspectives that have caused damage to people. Throughout history, people representing different faiths have done a substantial amount of harm in the name of religion. Elements of certain beliefs and religious practices can be seen as harsh, controversial, blasphemous or dangerous from the perspective of other worldviews. Some representatives of religion are not always as 'saintly' as they appear. It is hoped that the majority of sites and authors reviewed in this Guide are safe, pacific and user-friendly in imparting their knowledge to the wider world, although that would depend on the individual reader's perspective (see the Safe Surfing section).

As with hypertext, you don't need to follow a linear path when reading this Guide. For ease of access, however, it is divided into four main sections, which are not intended to be hierarchical: General Portals on Faith introduces specialist entry points which can be effectively used to seek out knowledge about religion; World Religions covers Buddhism, Christianity, Hinduism, Islam, and Judaism; Other Beliefs introduces worldviews from diverse religious and spiritual perspectives; Contexts and Categories explores the phenomena associated with different dimensions of religion. There is also an Index, if you are looking for a specific aspect of world religions.

For the purposes of this book, 'religion' may be personal and individual in nature, and/or formal and institutional. It can be represented in many ways, and it is hoped that this Guide represents that rich diversity of human and sacred expression. Elements of controversy and evolving beliefs have been highlighted in this book, in particular where approaches to new forms of experience, knowledge and interpretation have been addressed. The serious life and death concerns tackled by some websites are also reviewed in this Guide, including those that have a strong religious-socio-political edge to them. In between these factors, there are some profoundly moving and spiritually uplifting areas of the internet, demonstrating the importance of religion to individual and community lives.

A site's inclusion does not imply personal endorsement by the writer of this Guide, who prefers not to engage in dialogues regarding the 'superiority' of one worldview to another. I could never be perceived as neutral, but I do not have membership or formal affiliation with any religion, either in this Guide or elsewhere. As a university lecturer, I have broad interests in world religions (particularly Islam) and associated phenomena, especially how technology changes the nature of religious expression and experience. Religion on the internet is a dynamic and evolving phenomenon, and it is an exciting time of change and transformation within the medium. There are some religions that are under-represented by quality sites in English, and I hope that this situation will improve in the not-too-distant future. New reviews and updates will be placed on the website, and your contributions are welcome. Please don't hesitate to send comments and suggestions, and enjoy surfing the divine.

safe surfing

It is recognised that there are belief systems with 'hate' agendas, ones that actively attack specific sections of society. Some of these are referred to in this Guide, with their selection based on the criterion of topicality, such as Aum Shinrikyo. After some consideration, it was decided not to include so-called 'suicide cults' such as Heaven's Gate and the Order of the Solar Temple, and sites associated with the Jonestown mass-suicide (although these are easy to access on the web through the General Portals section of this book).

This guide encourages readers to visit as many different online religious perspectives as possible, while noting that there are sites where some care might be needed if the reader decides on personal interaction with adherents. Dangers may simply be having one's email box flooded with polemical materials, or email address circulated onto other email lists without permission. Even the Patron Saint of the internet, St Isidore of Seville, may not be able to intercede when your system buckles under the strain of unsolicited mail. Avoid giving out personal details to individuals or organisations unless you are totally confident about them, especially if you decide to visit chatrooms or join emailing lists. Think about using an alias, at least until you are familiar and confident with an individual or organisation, and consider using a separate email address for this type of interaction. If you are purchasing a product through a site listed in this Guide, ensure that there is secure online ordering (and that it is activated!), and that you exercise the same caution when giving out financial details that you would within any other area of the internet.

If you are in any doubt about a religious group or organisation, whether it is linked to the 'mainstream' or not, do obtain independent advice or information, which can be found online. They cannot answer personal enquiries, but information about beliefs is located on the Religious Movements or Ontario Consultants on Religious Tolerance websites, both of which are reviewed in this Guide. Various religious and secular organisations attempt to provide their own forms of advice, and inevitably some are less than impartial (depending on your perspective). In Britain, INFORM (Information Network Focus on Religious Movements) aims to provide 'objective accurate, up to date information about new religions', especially new movements in established religions, and alternate religions. Based in the London School of Economics, INFORM is backed by the Home Office and mainstream churches, and has recently introduced a website (http://www.inform.ac) containing information about its agenda and activities. INFORM can be emailed for advice (inform@lse.ac.uk), and their telephone information line is open between 10.30am-4.30pm on 0207 955 7654.

These sources have their critics (especially on the web), and there are different understandings of independence and impartiality. Treat personal contact with individuals and groups in the same way as you would other aspects of the internet, being aware that there are a small percentage of people associated with some 'religious sites' on the internet who are particularly skilled in engaging individuals and manipulating them towards aims that do not necessarily fit conventional understandings of religion.

technical note

I have used a variety of computers and software over the past 20 years, from machines the size of bus shelters to the most portable of PCs. I had a conversion experience from Macs to PCs several years ago. It wasn't voluntary but I have yet to be de-programmed. In preparing this book, I initially surfed used early versions of browsers and platforms, so I can appreciate the frustration when encountering elements of site design that become inaccessible for all but elite users! To get the best from this Guide, I am hoping that readers will be using one of the latest browsers. At the time of writing, Microsoft's Internet Explorer 5.5 was winning the popularity battle against Netscape's latest offering, Communicator 6, with a new beta version of Explorer being tested. The Opera browser is an effective alternative. If you are using an old and reliable browser, and don't want to upgrade, don't panic: a significant proportion of the sites reviewed here will still be accessible.

Other software tools that I found useful were the latest RealPlayer 8, which can be used to access the majority of audio and video files found on the net. QuickTime was also helpful. Acrobat Reader was useful for downloading PDF files, which are usually longer documents presented in the conventional form of a book. Some of us could probably live without the Macromedia Flash plug-in, which is useful only if you want to see the dynamic animation concepts presented by some sites. Versions of all of these software options, from browser to plug-in, can be found inexpensively through the web, although the best way to acquire them is to purchase one of the many computer magazines with a software CD attached. It is quicker, cheaper and more effective to download software offline. Do virus-check the disk first, and ensure when browsing the web that your virus-checking software is up-to-date!

Dr Gary Bunt, June 2001

Acknowledgements

My wife Yvonne provided invaluable inspiration and support during the preparation of this book, while Kane Richard delivered his special form of editorial input. Other members of my family, in particular Tony and my parents, Betty and Derek, offered encouragement during this book's genesis. The support of colleagues at the University of Wales, Lampeter, is acknowledged. Thanks also to the team at the Good Web Guide for their support.

Gary Bunt, May 2001

Chapter 01

general portals on faith

The writing about and classification of religions has taken many forms over the years, ranging from the experiential to the scientific. A good library on religion would incorporate many of these viewpoints on its shelf, deeming that they all have a place when exploring the religions of the world. All religions also have a place on the internet, although they are not always as easy to locate as within a conventional library, and the quest for enlightenment in cyberspace also has many guises. Whether you are looking for a religion-related commercial product, or the shrine of an obscure saint, this section contains some of the best entry points for surfing on religion-related subjects, whatever your perspective on beliefs. The casual agnostic explorer and the dedicated theologian will both be able to utilise the resources gathered in this section in different ways.

It does help if you know what you looking for, although these sites are also useful for some general browsing! Some have alternative perspectives on shared subject matter, so comparative use of these resources may be interesting. Others follow a magazine-style format, frequently updated, and with opportunities for interactivity. These commercially oriented sites are fun to return to regularly, and you may find them useful introductory guides to religion in its various forms. There are also some high quality information resources produced both from the commercial and academic sectors, which can be helpful (depending on what you are looking for). The majority of these resources are searchable, and their navigation is straightforward. I have also included specialist sections of major search-engines, which can be applied to narrow the parameters, and point you in the 'right direction'. You may wish to place some of these sites on your Favourites, to return to them again. When using these General Portals, it may well be true that the passing of the journey is as enjoyable as the final destination.

www.beliefnet.com
Beliefnet

Overall rating: ★ ★ ★ ★			
Classification: Portal		**Readability:**	★ ★ ★ ★
Updating: Daily		**Content:**	★ ★ ★ ★ ★
Navigation: ★ ★ ★ ★		**Speed:**	★ ★ ★ ★ ★

US

This website has a busy and occasionally confusing front page, containing news about the site, articles, advertisements and sponsor details. They describe themselves as 'a multi-faith e-community designed to help you meet your own religious and spiritual needs – in an interesting, captivating and engaging way.' You can register through the top bar link if you wish to become a member, although it's not required for surfing the site. Benefits include newsletters and an email account. Ten Beliefnet zones are linked on the left-hand side bar, which is the best way to find your way around the site. Format is consistent throughout, with a Home link on each page taking you back to the start. There's even a tool to build your own website.

Beliefnet has a large shopping area for religious products, with secure credit card ordering. It can be difficult to distinguish between commercial and other site content.

SPECIAL FEATURES

Religions maintains the magazine format. When we visited, there was an interesting banner for Zen Jesus. Ranging from Bahai to Zoroastrianism, each section of the site contains discussions, interactive features and quizzes, online resources and links, and shopping links relating to each faith.

Spirituality has an ecumenical feel to it, with discussions and features from diverse faith perspectives. How to Yoga

and Angel Meditation were both interesting features, suggesting a new age edge to this section of the site.

Morality and Culture is particularly enjoyable for neutral surfers. We liked the Bishop's Top Films (Crouching Tiger, Hidden Dragon and Chicken Run scoring highly in 2000), Everyday Ethics (which solves moral dilemmas online), and the section on Science and Religion.

Beliefnet Dictionary is a searchable version of the HarperCollins Dictionary of Religion, written in 1995 by The American Academy of Religion. Either enter your chosen query into the search engine box, or run through the A-Z for an academic and exhaustive definition.

OTHER FEATURES

There's so much content here that you're bound to go back for seconds. Sections on Humour, Music, and News are also impressive. If you suffer information overload, which is quite likely however much stamina you have, then take a break and send a colourful Beliefnet electronic card.

Five stars for Beliefnet's imaginative and innovative content, although the advertising may alienate some readers.

http://religioustolerance.org/
Ontario Consultants on Religious Tolerance

Overall rating: ★ ★ ★ ★ ★			
Classification:	Information	**Readability:**	★ ★ ★ ★ ★
Updating:	Regularly	**Content:**	★ ★ ★ ★ ★
Navigation:	★ ★ ★	**Speed:**	★ ★

CAN

Ontario Consultants on Religious Tolerance have produced one of the premier resources on religious diversity, promoting their message of inclusiveness since 1995. The site has four authors, from different faith/no faith perspectives, and other contributors. It can be difficult to search the site for a particular area of interest, but persistence can pay dividends. Navigate using the side bar, which contains links to the main sections of the site. We found that the best navigation point was Your First Visit?, which explains hyperlinks to principal areas. A preponderance of GIFs and adverts, slows download times.

SPECIAL FEATURES

Cults: from positive to homicidal faith groups is a substantial hyperlinked essay that distinguishes between cults and other religious movements, and analyses the different reactions to different forms of faith.

Hot Topics approaches areas of conflict with a religious theme or background. It's a great place to read about medical ethics, sexuality and the occult. The most visited section is one on Nudism and Naturism, which the authors note does not contain any pictures.

Don't be dissuaded by the home-made quality of some pages, because the quality of the articles is extremely high, and (whatever your faith perspective) the site merits frequent visits.

www.religiousmovements.org
Religious Movements Homepage

Overall rating: ★ ★ ★ ★			
Classification:	Information	**Readability:**	★ ★ ★ ★ ★
Updating:	Regularly	**Content:**	★ ★ ★ ★ ★
Navigation:	★ ★ ★ ★	**Speed:**	★ ★ ★ ★

US

This is another classic entry point for general information about religion. The site is organised by an American academic, Jeffrey K Hadden. Although it can be defined as a scholarly site, there's a great deal for the curious general surfer, especially if you are new to exploring faith on the internet. Michelangelo inspired the front page, with classic images from the Sistine Chapel illuminating key zones of the site. There is an effective site map and a search engine. On main pages, there is a consistent page format consisting of a left-hand side bar with key hot links; articles and papers have a top bar for navigation.

SPECIAL FEATURES

Group Profiles offers an alphabetical listing of essays, many produced by students from the University of Virginia, profiling different religious groups, linking to selected web sites and providing suggested print resources. There are at least 200 groups listed. Alongside major world religions, there are some surprising inclusions, such as Alcoholics Anonymous and the Snake Handlers. The articles vary in quality, but are generally authoritative and well referenced, although there are some broken links for selected websites.

OTHER FEATURES

The Group Profiles can also be accessed via listings of Faith Traditions and Religious Family Groupings. There are also

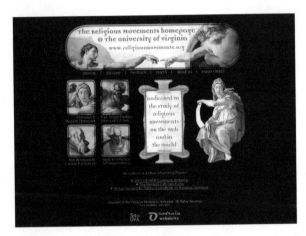

interesting sections on Religious Broadcasting and Religious Freedom.

This is an important, well-presented and encyclopedic site containing an overwhelming amount of quality information, and you may find it easier to print off specific articles rather than read them online.

http://about.com/religion/

About – Religion/Spirituality

Overall rating: ★ ★ ★ ★

Classification:	Portal	**Readability:**	★ ★ ★ ★
Updating:	Daily	**Content:**	★ ★ ★ ★
Navigation:	★ ★ ★ ★ ★	**Speed:**	★ ★ ★ ★ ★

US

Although there are many fine religion portals on the internet, designed to provide a quick entry point into the diversity of cyberspirituality, About's site is particularly easy to navigate. It also leads into other pages produced by the commercial site which describes itself as the Human Internet. All About sites follow a standard format, and here you'll find specialist religion pages on principal religions and related subjects. They can vary in quality, but all have associated newsletters, available by email subscription, and informative hosts. Front pages are changed regularly, to incorporate news and features. Navigate via the search engine at the top of the page, or visit one of the sections highlighted on the front page.

SPECIAL FEATURES

Alternative Religions seeks to define cults, sects and religious movements, and also contains a great section on African Religions.

Agnosticism/Atheism is lively and well informed. Host Austin Cline has produced definitions of the key terms. The Discussion Forum and Atheism Chat can be highly charged, with people from different faith (and other) perspectives engaging in dynamic dialogue.

Live Chat on various religious subjects (details at the bottom of the front page) takes place every week, to which you can contribute. Timings are Eastern Standard Time; to check the

time difference, use the Time Zone Clocks website (www.town-usa.com/timezoneworldclocks.html) .

About – Religion/Spirituality is certainly what can be described as a sticky site, to be returned to frequently, and the primary disadvantage would seem to be a danger of information overload, and the intrusive (religious and non-religious) advertisements throughout.

http://brittanica.com
Britannica

Overall rating: ★ ★ ★ ★			
Classification:	Encyclopedia	Readability:	★ ★ ★
Updating:	Regularly	Reliability:	★ ★ ★ ★
Navigation:	★ ★ ★	Speed:	★ ★ ★ ★

US

The online version of the Encyclopaedia Britannica is a useful place to search for 'neutral' information about religions, in historical, cultural and contemporary contexts. Unless you know specifically what you are looking for, the entry point is best located through typing in 'religion' on the front page search engine. This takes you through to a magazine-style page on religion, where there's a column on religion-related websites, selected encyclopedia entries, magazines and related products. All the articles are exhaustive, and great places to study more about religions. The content is anything but superficial, although its density may dissuade some casual surfers.

SPECIAL FEATURES

Search Engine is highly effective, and is the best method of surfing the site. A test search on 'Rastafarian' located four website reviews, a couple of paragraphs about the religion, and links to Bob Marley and reggae articles. Searching under 'Buddhism' located 11 articles, four website reviews, and a substantial number of related products. You may have reservations about the representative quality of some of the websites selected.

The fact that the site wants to sell you the encyclopedia (and other products) shouldn't put you off taking a tour if you are searching for information about a particular faith or practice.

http://directory.google.com/Top/Society/Religion_and_Spirituality/			
Google – Religion and Spirituality			
Overall rating: ★ ★ ★ ★			
Classification:	Search Engine	**Readability:**	★ ★ ★
Updating:	Daily	**Reliability:**	★ ★ ★ ★
Navigation:	★ ★ ★ ★	**Speed:**	★ ★ ★ ★ ★
US			

Google have created a substantial listing of thousands of sites related to religion, with some limited explanatory information. While being comprehensive, it can also be intimidating, even for seasoned surfers. Thankfully, the search engine can be directed specifically to this subject area, so the site can be useful if you are looking for something very particular.

SPECIAL FEATURES

Shopping lists the substantial range of faith-related online stores, breaking them down into religious categories, and highlighting shops whose clientele transcend religious barriers.

Religious Studies contains a useful one-page summary of important general portals. Be aware that there can be substantial duplication between these sites.

Google is a quick method of locating useful information about faith, although general surfers may prefer more user-friendly interfaces.

http://religion.rutgers.edu/vri/index.html			
Virtual Religion			
Overall rating: ★ ★ ★ ★			
Classification:	Portal	**Readability:**	★ ★ ★
Updating:	Regularly	**Reliability:**	★ ★ ★ ★
Navigation:	★ ★ ★	**Speed:**	★ ★ ★ ★
US			

This specialist academic site from Rutgers University, New Jersey, is a major catalogue of online religion, which is easy to navigate and comprehensive in content. The main page is also the site map, listing zones and outlining their key areas. If you are looking for a specialist topic relating to faith, then this is a great place to look. Each page links to an annotated listing of important websites within a subject area, and has hyperlinks to other sections of the site on the top of the page. Many of these are scholarly in orientation, and there is a North American bias to many of the recommended links.

SPECIAL FEATURES

Psychology of Religion is a useful introduction to the subject, with links to classic texts, a conceptual framework relating to religious experience, and work on Jung and Freud.

Ethics and Moral Values is an excellent hyperlinked page, highlighting important resources on moral theory, criminal and social justice, life and death issues, sex and gender issues, welfare and environment, and war and peace. All of human life is here!

OTHER FEATURES

All world religions are represented on this site, although some pages are better developed than others. Pages on

Confessional Agencies and Comparative Religion are worth visiting.

For serious surfers, this is a great portal into the academic study of religion.

www.bbc.co.uk/religion/
BBC Online – Religion and Ethics

Overall rating: ★ ★ ★			
Classification:	Information	**Readability:**	★ ★ ★
Updating:	Regularly	**Reliability:**	★ ★ ★
Navigation:	★ ★ ★	**Speed:**	★ ★ ★

(UK)

Some say that the BBC were under pressure to produce this site to complement their exhaustive and often exemplary web coverage in other areas. First placed online in 2001, this site introduces basic information on faith, combined with the latest religion news and material from BBC broadcasts. Navigate via the side bar, which takes you to the main zones of the site. The strength of this site lies in links to original BBC content from radio and television.

SPECIAL FEATURES

Thought for the Day contains a RealPlayer archive of the past week's short radio talks, reflecting diverse faith perspectives.

What the Papers Say summarises content from the religious press, and contains a useful listing of media URLs.

OTHER FEATURES

Guide to the UK's Main Religions offers a concise summary of Sikhism, Christianity, Islam, Judaism, Hinduism and Buddhism, which may be useful for comparative purposes.

When reviewed, Religion and Ethics was still in an early incarnation, and while helpful for religion news, the site's full potential has yet to be realised.

OTHER SITES OF INTEREST

Adherents
www.adherents.com/
Adherents contains statistical information on over 4,200 religions. The site is regularly updated. Material is available through the site's A-Z listing, or by listings of world religions by size, major branches, world's largest churches, and other parameters.

Internet Resources for the Study and Teaching of Theology
http://info.ox.ac.uk/ctitext/theology/
This is a comprehensive, academically oriented, annotated listing of theology resources that is very useful for scholars of different faiths, and Christianity in particular.

Religion Online
www.religion-online.org
When Religion Online's founder, William Fore, identified an absence of online books about religion, he set about remedying the situation by placing more than 2,100 articles and chapters onto the web. There's a wide range of topics, including the Bible, comparative religion, religious communication, and religious education. The site's front page is categorised into principal sections, although if you are seeking out something specific there is also a search engine.

Voice of the Shuttle: Religious Studies Page
http://vos.ucsb.edu/shuttle/religion.html
This long-standing traditional listing of websites (without much explanation) can be found at the Voice of the Shuttle.

Yahoo!
(http://dir.yahoo.com/Society_and_Culture/Religion_and_Spirituality/)
Yahoo! provides a similar exhaustive listing to Google on Religion and Spirituality, although the search parameters are different. It's easy to get lost in this directory, and some of the links were broken when we tested the site.

Still stuck?

See the Further Surfing section of this book.

want to read **more reviews** on this subject?

log on to

www.thegoodwebguide.co.uk

world religions

This chapter contains sections on Buddhism, Christianity, Hinduism, Islam and Judaism. The Christianity section is somewhat larger than others, due to an overwhelming diversity of materials available to browse online. This should not detract from the fact that the other world religions in this chapter also provide excellent resources, and in a larger volume it would have been possible to list hundreds of sites associated with each belief.

The growth in internet usage outside of the 'western' sphere will influence the quantity and quality of religion sites during the next decade, as greater opportunities emerge for self-expression and propagation, and awareness of the potential of the net increases. The globalisation and dispersal of believers has led to authoritative religious sites appearing in minority' contexts, or materials for sites being drawn from contributors across the world. Social and cultural aspects of religious beliefs are well represented on several sites, even to the extent of offering matchmaking services. There is also a level of political activism on some of these religious sites, with significant issues of belief being discussed through the electronic medium.

The past few years has seen a race to get online between and within the world religions outlined in this chapter. There has been religion-related content on the internet ever since the technology first appeared. People representing different world religions subsequently decided that they wanted a slice of the action, as they became aware of the propagation, networking, and outreach possibilities of the web. It is also a relatively inexpensive way to reach a lot of people. Within some religions, there were concerns that 'unofficial' sites may misrepresent the official offices, and in some cases that 'anti-religion' sites were gaining an upper hand.

Whatever the motivations, the result has been a sustained effort from some groups to produce pages fully representing their worldview. This effort has, in some cases, also incorporated useful search-engine and navigation tools, and a broad range of subject matter and resources. There have been a few disasters as well, particularly in terms of long download speeds, broken links and poor interactive options. Gradually, depending on the resources of a religious group, the homegrown qualities of some sites has been replaced by a professional awareness of web design. This has advantages in terms of effective access to information, but at times the idiosyncratic and quirky nature of some sites has been replaced by a homogeneous and boring uniformity.

Official sites are often better resourced. They may contain regularly updated materials, and some outline appropriate prayers and religious activities for every day of the year. Away from the corporate images of central offices, you will still find websites produced by individual adherents that present a personal view of their belief, occasionally illustrated by unique images. There can also be a high level of interaction, and insight into the spiritual motivations for a particular belief. Take your pick from the selection in this chapter, which contain some of the best belief-centred resources available online. Even if you disagree with a certain perspective, the clarity and information value of many of these sites should offer something even to the most hardened sceptic.

buddhism

www.buddhanet.net
BuddhaNet

Overall rating: ★ ★ ★ ★ ★			
Classification: Information		**Readability:**	★ ★ ★ ★
Updating: Regularly		**Reliability:**	★ ★ ★ ★ ★
Navigation: ★ ★ ★ ★ ★		**Speed:**	★ ★ ★ ★

(AUS)

Organised by the Buddha Dharma Education Association in Sydney, BuddhaNet describes itself as a 'non-sectarian organisation'. Look upon the site as a free library, primarily downloads of the printed word, although there are some beautiful visual resources as well. It might take some months to fully explore the contents of BuddhaNet, given that it covers so many aspects of Buddhism in detail. Not only is this site an invaluable introduction to Buddhism, but those with prior knowledge of the subject will find much of benefit within its pages. You'll need an Acrobat reader, MP3 player, and WinZip software to be able to access all the content of the site. There is little in the way of pure HTML content, aside from the fascinating and detailed indices of material.

Click on the golden prayer wheel that greets you on arriving at BuddhaNet, and you arrive at the contents listing, adjacent to a gold statue of the contemplative Buddha. This image is a substantial file, which can take some time to assemble itself, but is worth the wait, as 15 hyperlinked categories are revealed. This includes a link to a search engine, in case you know what you are seeking. These are the main sections of the site, and this page is the one you'll

return to if you click on Home anywhere in the site. BuddhaNet is a joy to surf, being easy to navigate with a consistent style. All the site's links are all fully functional, which means you can focus on content and design rather than technical issues.

SPECIAL FEATURES

E-Books contains a listing of more than 40 PDF files (sizes given) on a broad range of topics. If your Acrobat reader is already installed, then all you have to do is click on your title of choice. Some files are also available as printable zip files (although the Acrobat files can easily be printed too). E-Books is divided into sections on General Buddhism, Buddhist Meditation and Buddhist Studies. If you are new to Buddhism, then start with 'Good Question, Good Answer', which has basic introductory questions on Buddhist concepts. Then take a look at 'Four Noble Truths', which introduce the central teachings of Buddhism, and the classic text 'Buddhism in a Nutshell'. These books provide useful gateways into understanding Buddhism. Essentially they are reproductions of pamphlets, so may be easiest to download and read in printed form offline. You can always return to the listing for more reading(!).

File Library is outstanding, being divided into areas of different forms of Buddhism, with extensive listings on Theravadan, Mahayana, Tibetan, and Chan Buddhism in the form of downloadable files, texts, and resources. These are aimed at different levels of interest and understanding, and are clearly explained in the listing. If you've had enough of reading, then recommended are the Buddha Art Files, containing at least 100 images downloadable as GIFs or zip files. These are classic good quality images from diverse Buddhist settings and contexts, listed with file size, although no indication of copyright control. The writer enjoyed 'Dorje: The thunderbolt that destroys ignorance', 'The Buddha's Enlightenment', and 'Wheel of Life'. Also recommended in the File Library are the archived audio files, in MP3 and WAV formats (together with text transcriptions as zips). These contain Buddhist chanting, with small files of the Mantra Om Mani Padme Hum, which give you a flavour before tackling lengthier extracts from the Chanting Book of Western Australia. Some of these files are very large (up to 5.1MB), so be prepared for a long period of contemplation prior to listening. There is also meditation instruction, in audio and text formats. Elsewhere in the File Library, there are materials that can be downloaded for a Palm Pilot, and text books for use by Primary and Secondary Students.

OTHER FEATURES

The site contains an international listing of hospices, and extensive directories of Buddhist organisations. There is also a regularly updated Top Ten listing of Buddhist websites.

The reliance on PDF rather than HTML may be seen as a drawback by some surfers, but if you are a traveller on the path of enlightenment, or simply curious, then the extensive resources contained on BuddhaNet should answer your questions on this thoughtful and well-designed site.

www.ratanagiri.org.uk/
Aruna Ratanagiri: Harnham Buddhist Monastery

Overall rating: ★ ★ ★ ★			
Classification:	Information	**Readability:**	★ ★ ★ ★
Updating:	Regularly	**Reliability:**	★ ★ ★
Navigation:	★ ★ ★ ★	**Speed:**	★ ★ ★ ★ ★

UK

Harnham Buddhist Monastery, located on the remote Scottish-English border in Northumbria, is part of an international network of centres and monasteries associated with the Aruna Ratanagari community. The website provides details of monastery activities, and a downloadable collection of talks by the order's Thai founder Phra Ajahn Chah (1918-1992). The pages are easy to find, being listed on the front page. Other pages contain a link back to Home.

SPECIAL FEATURES

Publications include meditational teachings and an outline of Buddhism. Surfers can send a blank audio cassette to the order, and receive a tape of chanting by return. Unfortunately no soundfiles were available.

Eight Precepts outlines a daily routine that commences at five o'clock in the morning with the rising bell and chanting. It is possible to arrange visits and meditate at Harnham.

OTHER FEATURES

The site also produces a regular newsletter.

Harnham have produced an interesting online insight into Buddhist life in Britain.

www.dharmanet.org/
DharmaNet

Overall rating: ★ ★ ★ ★			
Classification:	Portal	**Readability:**	★ ★ ★ ★
Updating:	Regularly	**Reliability:**	★ ★ ★ ★
Navigation:	★ ★ ★ ★ ★	**Speed:**	★ ★ ★ ★ ★

US

Barry Kapke founded DharmaNet in 1991, and at the time of writing was seeking donations in order to develop the site further. DharmaNet is very user-friendly, as it contains few graphics, no sidebars, and is both searchable and easy to navigate.

SPECIAL FEATURES

The site is one of the best subject gateways to Buddhism on the internet, and is divided into three main sections. DharmaNet InfoWeb lists online Buddhism organisations, monasteries and practice centres. InterLinks contains academic materials and databases. Personal Pages are non-academic in orientation, with at least 150 links to diverse perspectives on Buddhism. This area of DharmaNet would be most useful for surfers wishing to develop their existing knowledge of Buddhism, especially if they know where they wish to travel on the path to enlightenment. There is a potentially useful online library, although it was inaccessible at the time of review. However, DharmaNet is not recommended as an introductory resource.

If there is a Zen guide to web design, then it is reflected in the site's simplicity, although the listing is most useful for those with a developed knowledge of Buddhism.

www.tibet.com/Buddhism/index.html
Tibetan Government in Exile – Tibetan Buddhism

Overall rating: ★ ★ ★ ★			
Classification:	Portal	**Readability:**	★ ★ ★
Updating:	Regularly	**Reliability:**	★ ★ ★ ★
Navigation:	★ ★ ★ ★	**Speed:**	★ ★ ★

IND

There is some fascinating content here relating to Tibetan Buddhism, although it is primarily textual in nature.

SPECIAL FEATURES

Articles on Buddhist hand gestures, and the monastic life for a western monk at Sera Je were particularly interesting. They included an interview with a German monk, Ven. Fedor Stracke. Find out why the monks shout as they debate, and what a typical monastic day is like.

OTHER FEATURES

The pages also contain general historical and religious information on Tibetan Buddhism, and links to an extensive annotated listing of the Dalai Lama's statements, together with biographical information.

The site is easy to navigate and provides a good base to further explore Tibetan economic, social and political concerns.

www.dalailama.com/

Dalai Lama

Overall rating: ★ ★ ★			
Classification:	Portal	**Readability:**	★ ★
Updating:	Regularly	**Reliability:**	★ ★ ★
Navigation:	★ ★ ★	**Speed:**	★ ★

(IND) (TIB) (US)

The entry page contains photos of the Dalai Lama from childhood through to the present day. Click on the photos to enter the site, dedicated to His Holiness Tenzin Gyatso, the 14th Dalai Lama of Tibet. The links on this page are not always clear, and lack labels. The top bar lists aspects of the Dalai Lama's life; Young Dalai Lama and Statesman link to biographical pages, illustrated with photos, but mostly text.

SPECIAL FEATURES

Spiritual Leader links to a choice of teachings, essentially a series of verses, and Publications introduces a listing of writings.

Peace and Non-violence displays the Dalai Lama's 1989 Nobel Prize speech, and an excerpt from his 'Ethics for a New Millennium' speech.

OTHER FEATURES

The contents page also links into a diary of the Dalai Lama's engagements, and to information about Tibet.

Surprisingly the site does not take full advantage of the internet, certainly in terms of reproducing the Dalai Lama's speeches and publications to a global audience, and is therefore in its present form something of a disappointment.

www.dechen.org/

Dechen Community – Karma Thinley Rinpoche

Overall rating: ★ ★ ★			
Classification:	Information	**Readability:**	★ ★ ★ ★
Updating:	Regularly	**Reliability:**	★ ★ ★
Navigation:	★ ★ ★ ★	**Speed:**	★ ★ ★ ★

(UK)

The Dechen Community is based on the Tibetan Sakya tradition, and its spiritual leadership under Karma Thinley Rinpoche and his Dharma-regent Lama Jampa Thaye. The site is well designed, and easy to navigate. The page style is consistent, with navigation via the top of the page, which lists the major areas of the site.

SPECIAL FEATURES

Karma Thinley Rinpoche describes his life and teachings, and the development of his centres throughout the world.

Karma Kagyu Tradition explains this form of Tibetan Buddhism, and the importance of the cycles of mahamudra (great seal) and the six doctrines. The issue of leadership succession is raised in the article, which includes photos of the young candidates 'recognised as the reincarnation of the sixteenth Karmapa and thus as the head of the Karma-Kagyu tradition'.

Centres and Groups provides a listing of its 20 centres in the United Kingdom.

Dechen Community have created a site more for specialists and devotees, but with plenty of information of general interest relating to the Buddhist belief system.

www.nichirenshoshu.or.jp/eng/indexe.html		
Nichiren Shoshu Buddhism		
Overall rating: ★ ★ ★		
Classification: Information	**Readability:**	★ ★ ★
Updating: Occasionally	**Reliability:**	★ ★ ★
Navigation: ★ ★ ★	**Speed:**	★ ★ ★ ★

This is a recent addition to Buddhist cyberspace, presenting 'official' information on this 750-year-old form of Buddhism. The site can be navigated by the side bars on the front page, or via links on the top of other pages. The page design is consistent.

SPECIAL FEATURES

Basics provides a brief Chronology of Nichiren Shoshu Buddhism, and an interesting calendar describing ceremonies throughout the year.

Head Temple Taisekiji is a fascinating cyber tour of the centre of Nichiren Shoshu Buddhism, located at Mount Fuji. The historical and religious significance of each area is described, and there are some beautiful photographs.

OTHER FEATURES

Topics, listed on the front page, provides recent news and photographs of activities at Taisekiji. Other areas of the site are still under construction. There is also a Japanese version of the site.

This is an interesting introduction into Nichiren Shoshu Buddhism, which will be worth returning to as the site develops.

www.abm.ndirect.co.uk/		
The Buddha Mind		
Overall rating: ★ ★ ★		
Classification: Information	**Readability:**	★ ★ ★
Updating: Regularly	**Reliability:**	★ ★ ★
Navigation: ★ ★ ★	**Speed:**	★ ★ ★ ★

This ambitious, user-friendly site makes good use of the internet as a teaching tool, although those still using early browsers may have some difficulty with some of the frames and animation. There is a sense that the designers wanted to play with as many design tools as they could; some of the results are successful and very original – if you know where to find them. Before loading the page, you may wish to turn your speakers off, to ignore the irritating MIDI file that accompanies the opening page. The page itself features a 'dissolving head' in cross-section, and offers a choice of different sides of the Buddha Mind: choose from Leftbrain (intellectual, academic, neat) or Rightbrain (casual, emotional, and spontaneous). The link to the Shrine Room is represented by an electric blue nothingness, appropriate within Buddhism perhaps, but not useful for the reader seeking information. However, better quality pages are provided elsewhere, and the site is worth persisting with, although several pages appear to be works in progress, complete with notes and musings from the authors.

SPECIAL FEATURES

Leftbrain contains a succinct explanation of Buddhism, which is a good introduction for 'newcomers'. It is easy to navigate and loads quickly, with a side bar linking to the main sections. Teachings include a summary of works spoken by the Buddha, but the best-developed section is Art and Culture, with features and images relating to symbols, shrines and architecture. Activities has a fascinating section on music and chanting in the Theravadan tradition, with MP3 examples ranging from monastic chanting to rap, which are used in educating children about Buddhism.

Rightbrain makes irritating use of javascript mouseover technology, in which the pointer can be directed to a section of a clickable human brain. To reach the Rightbrain menu quickly, click anywhere on the brain. Once inside the site, there is a side bar on the left, indicating areas of interest. These have unusual names, not necessarily indicative of contents, but all sections apply cartoons and animation to present interesting information about Buddhism. These pages integrate some Buddha images and aphorisms, particularly effective in the humorous Moondogs section. Click on Buddhabyte, and then Buddhism Icons, to be presented with a choice of 34 clickable tabs at the top of the page: each takes you to a page on basic Buddhism, illustrated with statues and other images, occasionally linked into more complex materials, including books.

OTHER FEATURES

Downloads (inside Leftbrain) offers Buddhism-related puzzles, soundfiles of chanting, screensavers, games, a monastery chanting book, and images; it also includes software and advice for those wanting to make their own graphics. The site authors have gone to some lengths to explain the nature of downloads, and also provide links to appropriate software required to read the downloads. The Buddha Mind also links to the Amaravati Buddhism Monastery, a Theravadin monastery based in Hertfordshire, England, which has an extensive set of pages.

An original and interesting set of pages, which are useful as an introduction to Buddhism, although navigation can be difficult, and some pages are frustratingly incomplete.

www.thebuddhistsociety.org.uk/
The Buddhist Society UK

Overall rating: ★ ★			
Classification:	Information	Readability:	★ ★
Updating:	Regularly	Reliability:	★ ★
Navigation:	★ ★ ★	Speed:	★ ★ ★

UK

These pages represent the activities of one of the oldest Buddhist societies in Europe, founded in 1924, which has interests in many forms of Buddhist expression. Main areas of the site are linked on the front page (to the right of the Buddha's head). Once inside the site, navigate from the links at the bottom of the page, by clicking on a hyperlinked lotus.

SPECIAL FEATURES

The Life and Teachings of the Buddha contains some basic information, with tasteful images, but the content of the pages is quite dry.

OTHER FEATURES

There are details of Buddhist Society activities and classes, academic extracts from the Middle Way journal, and information on printed publications. Unfortunately, the latter are only available for purchase, rather than free download.

The content is sparse, but useful if you want to become involved in Buddhist Society activities.

buddhist texts

(see also Sacred Texts)

Collection of Mahayana Buddhist Sutras in English

www.best.com/~mlee/

This is one of the most comprehensive link pages of Buddhist texts available online in English. The Chinese texts can also be viewed in GIF format on this site. All the titles are listed on the front page, together with advice on respecting texts. Index contains more than 60 links to different sutras. The title of the site stresses the Mahayana identity, but there are also some Theravadan texts available to read as well. The pages tend to be text rich, which make them quick to download, although often difficult to read on screen for a sustained period. Links are primarily to external sites. This site is easy to navigate, and is particularly useful if you want quick access to a Buddhist text, and want to compare different translations.

Zen Buddhism WWW Virtual Library

www.ciolek.com/WWWVL-Zen.html

This is an academically oriented site, but is one of the most accessible explanations of Zen Buddhism on the internet. It's essentially an annotated link page, in which the Zen sites listed are explained, and material is updated frequently. Navigate by the table of contents, at the top of each page.

Buddhist Studies and the Arts

www.artsci.wustl.edu/~rrscott/

There's a wealth of images and information relating to Buddhism and the arts on this site, which represents an expert introduction to diverse forms of online Buddhist artistic expression, and is regularly updated.

Zen Art by Monk SongYoon

www.syzenart.com/

Monk SongYoon, resident in the Hovel of 10,000 Smiles in Seoul, Korea, presents his personal view of enlightenment, illustrated by a selection of unique paintings. The contemplative GIFs can take some time to download. Each one can be enlarged to study, and the Monk can be contacted directly by email about his work. He also discusses his artistic quest on his well-designed but simple web pages.

have you registered for **free updates?**

log on to

www.thegoodwebguide.co.uk

christianity

Given the substantial number of Christian sites available, special features are only highlighted when they are truly significant developments. Otherwise, this section would be the size of the King James Bible.

anglicanism

www.church.co.uk/			
Oasis			
Overall rating: ★ ★ ★			
Classification: Information		**Readability:**	★ ★ ★
Updating: Regularly		**Reliability:**	★ ★ ★
Navigation: ★ ★ ★ ★		**Speed:**	★ ★ ★
UK			

Don't panic if you see an animated rodent in a wheel crossing your screen – it's just your browser loading up this Flash-centred site. There are a number of zones in God's House, including a Kitchen, Lounge, Study, and Attic. These are navigated via the left-hand side bar, which has the representation of a house on it (floors light up, determining specific areas). Be prepared for break-beat music, accompanying the rotating mouse.

SPECIAL FEATURES

Kitchen contains a fridge, with Food for Thought (a quote from Philip Larkin that wasn't about parents). One to One was more enlightening, with questions and answers on parenthood containing informed, sensible and, at-times amusing advice. The sense was that religion was pervading the pages, rather than being ladled on with a trowel.

Study incorporates four sections on the Bible, briefly comparing different translations and advising on using the text online. Bookcase has hyperlinks to several Christian titles. Letter rack facilitates the asking of questions to experts, who are not afraid even to answer questions from sadomasochists.

OTHER FEATURES

Lounge contains the topical God's House Magazine, and lively responses to the site (on the Sofa). Bedroom contains the thoughts of the site's own vicar. Hall is more directly religious, with information on the Alpha Course, the Christian Enquiry Agency, and the Y Foundation. The Bathroom was locked.

Still a work in progress, and somewhat over-conscious of its trendy animation, this site may build on its visual appeal when sufficient content becomes available.

www.england.anglican.org/
The Church of England

Overall rating: ★ ★ ★			
Classification:	hformation	**Readability:**	★ ★ ★
Updating:	Regularly	**Reliability:**	★ ★ ★
Navigation:	★ ★ ★	**Speed:**	★ ★ ★ ★ ★

UK

This is now a much improved and more dynamic site than its earlier versions, containing rich detail on the church. The purple and blue entry page fits neatly on the screen. Pass the cursor over eight hyperlinked categories in the middle of the page, and related icons appear to the right of the links. There is a lack of interactive opportunity on the site.

SPECIAL FEATURES

Liturgy contains an article that explains the origins of the common prayer, and links to morning, evening and night prayers (updated 365 days a year). These links can also be found in the side bar. Click on a category, and up pops the day's portion from a relevant text. If you get stuck, there's a section on how to pray.

About the Church of England incorporates useful sections on the historical background and origins of Christianity in Britain, the (Anglican perspective on the) Reformation, Relations with Other Faiths, and What it Means to be an Anglican.

OTHER FEATURES

The Gazette is a recent introduction, containing regular news from the Archbishop and other church offices.

The Church of England's site continues to improve, but can be rather cold and stuffy in places.

OTHER ANGLICAN SITES

Oremus
www.oremus.org/
'Oremus is a form of daily Christian prayer published on the internet. This website also contains resources for daily prayer and other worship, including hymns and liturgical forms.' Oremus makes good use of the technology, with innovative features including the Anglican Online Hymnal. Type in the words of a hymn, and out pops the title and full details. It successfully located 'All Things Bright and Beautiful' in seconds, and started playing the hymn on a MIDI sound file (sans vocal).

Church Net UK
www.churchnet.org.uk/
Church Net UK is a significant resource gateway, probably for more dedicated Anglican surfers, detailing many aspects of the Church of England in the UK. Among the pages are opportunities for prayer online, 'webchat' with other surfers, and submission of a question on religious issues.

Cyber Hymnal
http://tch.simplenet.com/
Taking the hymn concept one stage further, this site lists over 2,000 hymns by various criteria, including meter, scores, and trivia. The site is interdenominational, and certain tunes come in organ and other versions.

Episcopal Church, USA
www.ecusa.anglican.org/
The Church is linked to the Worldwide Anglican Communion, providing regularly updated news, and information for the Episcopal Church in the USA. The table of contents presents an interesting listing of over one hundred Anglican related resources.

Oxford Diocese, Church of England
www.oxford.anglican.org/
Many Anglican churches are establishing an online presence. This is one of the most longstanding and thorough sites, regularly updated, containing local information concerning the parish, a list of the Bishop's thoughts of the day, and opportunities to email the Diocesan Communications Officer with questions.

roman catholicism

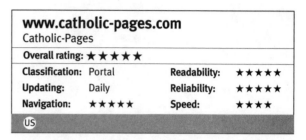

www.catholic-pages.com			
Catholic-Pages			
Overall rating: ★ ★ ★ ★			
Classification:	Portal	**Readability:**	★ ★ ★ ★ ★
Updating:	Daily	**Reliability:**	★ ★ ★ ★ ★
Navigation:	★ ★ ★ ★ ★	**Speed:**	★ ★ ★ ★
US			

If you seek specific information relating to Roman Catholicism on the internet, there are several effective portals to choose from. The easiest to navigate is Catholic-Pages, which is searchable, and with a well-organised directory of over 16,000 links to Catholicism on the web. There are no surprises in terms of its functional format, and the site is information rich rather than focused on design. All main categories are listed and linked on a table on the index page.

SPECIAL FEATURES

Theology is a substantial archive of downloadable archival documentation. The top of the page links to extensive sections on salvation, grace and justification, heaven, hell and purgatory, evolution and religious liberty. The writings of St Thomas Aquinas, St Augustine and the Doctors of the Church are also available. Further down the entry page, some of the classic works relating to Christianity and Catholicism are available to download. There is material to suit all levels of interest, from introductory onwards, and this section makes fascinating browsing. Hyperlinks may take you to other sites.

OTHER FEATURES

The rest of the site's content can be easily accessed through its entry page. Subject categories range from Catholic life and controversies, through to priests, nuns, and prayers. All of these lead to further hyperlinked listings, containing libraries of information. Catholic News Headlines are provided on the entry page on a daily basis. If this gets too heavy, try the Catholic jokes section. There is the (inevitable?) Good Books link to Amazon.com, featuring Catholic titles. If you wish, you can personalise this page with your favourite links. At the time of writing, the Word of the Day was Mortification.

Whether your interest is scholarly or general, Catholic-Pages has the capacity to lead you to the information you seek through its easy-to-navigate pages.

www.cin.org
Catholic Information Network

Overall rating: ★★★★			
Classification:	Information	Readability:	★★★★
Updating:	Daily	Reliability:	★★★★
Navigation:	★★	Speed:	★★★

US

The California-based Catholic Information Network (CIN) has promoted its 'electronic evangelisation' since 1987, and this experience shows in an information-rich resource that is a 'one-stop shop' for Catholicism. The site is not an official site of the Roman Catholic Church, but certainly effectively augments the church's other electronic resources. CIN itself has a sense of online mission, with its combination of email, chat, and regularly updated web-based resources. Key Catholic issues are highlighted on its opening page, including the Shroud of Turin, Contraception, and Abortion. CIN's content can at times be rather 'dry', requiring dedication and focus to wade through the substantial content.

At the time of writing, the introduction of applets (causing images and hyperlinks to change rapidly when the mouse pointer was placed on them) was making navigation confusing, although previous versions of the site were easier to get around, and this might just be a temporary glitch. A number of other 'improvements' have impaired navigability, and the site features the deadly sin of web design, of being best viewed using Internet Explorer 5. This is bad news for Netscape, Opera, and users of older versions of Explorer. The site really can be awkward for other browsers and older computers, although it looks better if you are lucky to have installed the correct software and are Java-enabled. Otherwise, navigation bars do not function properly, and the site can be frustrating.

Once inside the site's main pages, the designer has seen fit to use icons (of the computer variety) that lack ALT labels defining their destination, causing the reader to have to guess where the hyperlink might take them. The large images are picturesque, and in some cases hyperlinked to other parts of the site. The site is theoretically searchable, although that facility was 'down' at the time of writing. Hopefully, CIN's technical competence will be restored to its former glory once they have ironed out the problems of their makeover.

SPECIAL FEATURES

Pope John Paul II and the Vatican highlighted the activities of the Pope, detailing all of his statements, apostolic letters, prayers, homilies and news on papal visits. You might ask whether the Pope ever took a break, reading this exhaustive listing, which dates back to 1992, and gives every formal statement of his Holiness an instant platform in cyberspace. Materials from the 1992-95 period can also be obtained via FTP/ZIP files. While there are some parallels with the Vatican's own site, some extra materials can be located on these pages; details of papal audiences, and Sunday Angelus message, are also published. Provide CIN with your email address, and they will update you regularly with similar materials. New material is added daily.

Mailing List Directory CIN was established around the mailing lists, and this directory provides a comprehensive hyperlinked listing containing 52 different discussion forums. You can join as many as you wish, simply to read the contents, or to make active contributions. This listing gives CIN an edge over much of the Catholic internet competition, with its moderated discussions on different issues connected with Catholicism, with titles ranging from Natural Family Planning to Ask Father (is there a connection here?).

CIN Message Boards are extensive, and include Prayer Intentions, which can be emailed and shared with others, In Memoriam, Apologetics, Funstuff (including Jokes and Anecdotes – 'G-Rated'), and Book and Movie Reviews. This interactivity is a real strength of CIN, and not all Message Boards require membership, although their content is moderated.

OTHER FEATURES

Daily Word is a selection of daily Bible readings and commentaries appropriate for the day (highlighting specific feasts, saints' days, and other religious calendar occasions). Click the hyperlink for the day of the week you wish to study. Approximately 3,000 words in length (per day), their content will also be sent daily to readers via email by request, and are 'intended primarily towards personal reflection on the Word of God'.

Catholic News represents another of CIN's strengths. A Daily Dispatch includes the latest headlines from the Vatican, world features, and statements of the day from the Pope. Material is archived and searchable. The news is mirrored from the Zenit News Agency in Rome (www.zenit.org), and also available by email subscription.

Calendar details the biographies of saints, based upon their 'days', and introduces concise and interesting hagiographic résumés. Click on the calendar to discover the saint of the day.

St. Gabriel Gift and Book Nook sponsors this site. It also promotes a long list of Catholic materials, including software. Secure ordering is available, and you can test to determine whether you possess a compatible browser.

Regularly updated resources, together with useful news links and interactivity options, make this site an important Roman Catholic channel. CIN requires technical improvement to fulfil its potential for all visitors (whatever their browser!).

www.vatican.va/phome_en.htm
Vatican: The Holy See

Overall rating: ★ ★ ★			
Classification:	Information	**Readability:**	★ ★ ★
Updating:	Regularly	**Reliability:**	★ ★ ★
Navigation:	★ ★	**Speed:**	★ ★ ★ ★

ITA

Direct from Vatican City, this is the official papal website. Pope John Paul II (himself a silver surfer) endorsed the validity of information technology, and its potential applications for the Roman Catholic Church: 'Surely we must be grateful for the new technology which enables us to store information in vast man-made artificial memories, thus providing wide and instant access to the knowledge which is our human heritage...'.

This site is a work in progress, into which substantial resources are still being invested. Content is currently available in English, German, French, Portuguese, Spanish and Italian versions (with some Polish input). Upon loading, the pages look very inviting, with a classy (and uniform) parchment background. A series of Vatican symbols are arranged in a circular design surrounding the image of St. Peter's, and a hyperlink to The Holy Father. There are six smaller hyperlinked symbols; placing the mouse pointer on each will reveal the link it represents. Some guesswork is required on the English index page, as the site doesn't always follow conventional internet logic or fully explain where the hyperlinked images take the reader. The substantial amount of images used in the design impedes download times, although the final result is aesthetically pleasing. Perhaps some conventional labels and explanations would have improved accessibility.

Those lacking the patience to play hunt-the-hyperlink may decide that the Site Map link on the entry page would be the answer to their navigation prayers. Unfortunately, the link is broken. The FAQs link is also non-functional, but other hyperlinks on the second 'curve' of links (to the right of the images) lead to working areas of the site. This index page has a penitential feel, requiring readers to twist their heads to discern the full text. The Search link arrives at a high-powered engine that rapidly draws out material difficult to access through general browsing. This is best applied if the search parameters are kept fairly narrow (typing 'Pope' into the engine won't really help you!). Avoid clicking on the papal coat of arms on the top left-hand corner, unless you want to surf the site in another language, as this takes you to the universal entry page.

SPECIAL FEATURES

News Services provides formal press releases relating to the Pope, contained in the Bulletin of the Holy See, and links to other media. The Newspaper hyperlink connects to L'Osservatore Romano, a weekly Vatican newspaper available in English (and other languages). Radio offers links to Vatican Radio programmes via RealPlayer in over 40 languages and dialects. They invite you to 'Listen for Heaven's Sake!'. Check the Channel 1 hyperlink at the top of the page to confirm times of English broadcasts, or click Audio on Demand for the English language news schedule. This section also takes you to the Sunday Angelus Prayer. Television links to Centro Televisivo Vaticano, with live programmes and a Video Archive dating back to 1978 (under the Year in Review heading). The Angelus can also be viewed from different dates, and a selection of Audiences can be viewed (regularly updated). The Video Archive included Pope John Paul II opening the Holy Door of St Peter's for the Millennium celebrations, and highlights of Jubilees (some broken links). Download quality is reasonable via the RealPlayer format, although a choice of feed quality would have been useful.

The Holy Father, as one would expect, has a host of

resources online. Archives include encyclicals, apostolic letters, homilies, and speeches. If readers really want to discover what the Pope said to his audience, and on which day (and who was present), then there's a hyperlinked listing. The papal speeches and other exhortations given during his travels are given in full. This section also features a side bar listing the nine Popes from the 20th century. Clicking on a hyperlink presents a page on each, with the minimum of photo, papal coat of arms, and biographical details. The Holy Fathers have selected speeches, encyclicals, papal declarations and other materials represented online. Locating working hyperlinks is difficult here, as a significant amount of data still has to be entered into the site.

OTHER FEATURES

After discovering the working links, it is disappointing that some promised categories lack substantial content. It is possible to browse the Secret Archives (so secret that there's very little material currently online) and the Library (where you can view the catalogue). This site still seems to be in a developmental stage, notably the empty pages on the Museum and City State. There is little on the Swiss Guard at present, other than photos. The Synod of Bishops has a page of text, but no photos. The Index page also provides clear links to Liturgies and Paths of the Spirits – a selection of papal sermons based on St Augustine, St Anselm and others.

The Holy See website is a half-empty chalice, or half-full, depending on your perspective. Given time, the Vatican site may truly represent all the activities of the sacred city, but at present the site is best viewed as an authoritative resource on the Pope.

www.catholic-forum.com/saints/indexsnt.htm
Patron Saints' Index

Overall rating: ★ ★ ★			
Classification:	Encyclopedia	**Readability:**	★ ★ ★ ★
Updating:	Occasionally	**Reliability:**	★ ★ ★ ★
Navigation:	★ ★ ★ ★	**Speed:**	★ ★ ★ ★ ★

US

Part of the Catholic Forum site, this is an effective and user-friendly searchable index of over 2,000 saints, listed by topic, name, and nationality. The right-hand sidebar contains hyperlinks to image galleries, saints news, FAQs and various email lists. The categories under which saints can be located are intriguing.

SPECIAL FEATURES

Disease related will delight hypochondriacs, containing a list of 97 topics ranging from 'against earache' through to 'wounds': pick a malady and find an appropriate saint!

Animals came up with St. Blaise of Armenia (complete with picture and biography) when searching for recourse against 'wild beasts.'

OTHER FEATURES

There is also a hyperlinked Timeline, so saints can be sought by century.

This is a fascinating resource, making good use of web technology, helpful for those wanting to learn more about hagiography.

htpp://redslimerick.homepage.com
Redemptorists, Mount St. Alphonsus, Limerick City

Overall rating: ★ ★ ★ ★			
Classification: Information		**Readability:**	★ ★ ★
Updating: Regularly		**Reliability:**	★ ★ ★ ★
Navigation: ★ ★ ★ ★		**Speed:**	★ ★ ★ ★

(UK)

The Redemptorists (Congregation of the Most Holy Redeemer) at Mount St. Alphonsus, Limerick, Ireland, have produced a detailed and well-designed site based around the activities of their community of brothers and priests. When exploring their pages, be prepared for MIDI sound files to open. Some of these are atmospheric, and the use of bells to greet the reader on the index page is original (irritating if you need to keep returning there).

SPECIAL FEATURES

The Prayer Pot offers a substantial choice of sacred contemplative materials. A recording of the Sunday Night Mass (via Windows Media Player) is available.

Our Mother of Perpetual Help explains the history behind an important Redemptorist artefact.

OTHER FEATURES

This site also links to substantial other resources.

The impression of a dynamic community is conveyed through these pages, illustrated by a variety of paintings and images.

www.benedictine.net/
Benedictine Network

Overall rating: ★ ★ ★			
Classification: Portal		**Readability:**	★ ★ ★
Updating: Daily		**Reliability:**	★ ★ ★ ★
Navigation: ★ ★ ★		**Speed:**	★ ★ ★ ★

(US)

This is one of the best-organised and designed sites relating to a religious order, if you ignore the piano music that greets you on arrival. This extensive resource on the Benedictine Order provides information on religious houses, saints, apologetics, and reference materials.

SPECIAL FEATURES

Daily Readings and the **Liturgy of the Hours** are incorporated into a Universalis section: 'This site does all the calendar calculations for you, and presents you with the psalms and readings for each hour of today, every day.' Your time will never be your own again.

OTHER FEATURES

The site offers free email (yourname@benedictine.net) and chat. At the time of browsing, the question of whether Martin Luther King (a Protestant) should be considered for sainthood was under discussion on the site. The occasional advertising banner (such as the one for Christian lonely hearts) occasionally distracts from the spiritual dimensions of this site.

The Benedictine Network provide a detailed and interesting overview of the Order's activities on this regularly updated site.

www.fatima.org/
Fatima Network

Overall rating: ★ ★ ★

Classification:	Information	Readability:	★ ★ ★
Updating:	Occasionally	Reliability:	★ ★ ★
Navigation:	★ ★ ★	Speed:	★ ★ ★ ★

ITA

Fatima Network have produced a well-designed site, dominated by a representation of Our Lady of Fatima, and featuring the Java-based Perpetual Rosary through which readers can join in with prayers on the internet. The site campaigned for the Pope to publicly release the Third Secret of Fatima, and whether he bowed to cyber-pressure or not, the secret was released in May 2000. What is it all about? The Secret can be discovered in these pages, although the Vatican has attempted to suppress its message. Also available in Spanish, Portuguese, Italian and French flavours.

SPECIAL FEATURES

Prayer includes an opportunity for personal consecration (via email, submitting '[T]his pledge does not bind under penalty of sin, but nevertheless it is your promise to Our Blessed Lady').

Virtual Pilgrimage can be made to the places associated with Fatima, which was the location of a visitation by the Virgin Mary to three shepherd children in Portugal, during 1917.

Detailed information on Fatima combined with interactive and experimental elements, which make good use of net technology.

www.padrepio.com/
Padre Pio Foundation of America

Overall rating: ★ ★ ★

Classification:	Information	Readability:	★ ★ ★
Updating:	Regularly	Reliability:	★ ★ ★
Navigation:	★ ★ ★ ★	Speed:	★ ★ ★ ★

US

This site forms part of the active campaign seeking the canonisation of Padre Pio (1887-1968), who was beatified by Pope John Paul II in 1999. The site opens with images of the Padre, and quotations directed towards his 'Spiritual Children'.

SPECIAL FEATURES

The account of a Pilgrimage to Italy for the Beatification of Padre Pio introduces a personal note of spirituality, with pilgrims' photographs and journal entries.

OTHER FEATURES

The site is easy to navigate: scroll down the page to find links to sections on his Early Life, Stigmata, Sacraments, and Teachings. These pages load quickly, and lead primarily to archive photographs and brief articles. The Foundation runs a Bookstore and Giftshop, although at present only takes orders by phone or fax. A free Prayer Card is available, and you can join a Padre Pio Mailing List for further updates on the canonisation process.

Topical and regularly updated, this is an interesting introduction to Padre Pio, although it lacks depth in places.

http://viacrucis.org.uk/home.html
Via Crucis

Overall rating: ★ ★			
Classification:	Information	Readability:	★ ★
Updating:	Regularly	Reliability:	★ ★
Navigation:	★ ★ ★	Speed:	★ ★

UK

There's a long download time for this UK Catholic community website for 'strong Catholics', which seeks to introduce more UK-produced Catholic content onto its site. The design is cluttered, and contains flashing banners and images, but that should not distract too much from the detailed content.

SPECIAL FEATURES

Site Index, accessible from the main page, is helpful and searchable, allowing access to Reference, Action, Media, Topical, Faith and Practice, and Education sections.

Question and Answer Board allows non-Catholics wanting to find out more about the Church to send questions to Father Stephen.

OTHER FEATURES

Some of the site's content requires membership registration, which is free at present. Members can obtain a @catholic.uk.com email address and a free website. A Jubilee Indulgence can also be gained, using the guidance available on this site.

Via Crucis could do with a site overhaul, so that their interesting content is made more accessible.

OTHER CATHOLIC SITES

Archdiocese of Dublin
www.dublindiocese.ie
This 'unofficial site' is a useful starting point for those seeking Irish Catholic resources, with sections on Bishops, vocations, and regularly updated news. Navigate via an extensive links page containing homily helps, prayer sites, and more than 50 hyperlinks to other Catholic websites in Ireland and elsewhere (including parishes).

Carmelite Literature
www.ocd.or.at/lit/eng.htm
Teresa of Avila, John of the Cross, Edith Stein and other significant works are listed and linked.

Catholic Church in England and Wales
www.tasc.ac.uk/cc
This 'official' site is somewhat dry, but easy to navigate, and features news (in the form of occasional press releases), a hyperlinked listing of dioceses, and links to a prayer resource (the Liturgy Office has the unfortunate URL www.liturgy.demon.co.uk). Background information from the Catholic Media Office enlightens the reader on perspectives relating to topics such as homosexuality, celibacy, and capital punishment.

Catholic Encyclopedia
www.newadvent.org/cathen/
Nearly 12,000 articles are contained on these ambitious pages, which should answer many questions relating to the Roman Catholic Church. The original Encyclopedia was produced in 1913. The site relates how the project to place the Catholic Encyclopedia began in 1995, with hundreds of volunteers (including a cloistered nun) transcribing the entries, which were then converted into HTML. This is still a fascinating work-in-progress, well worth returning to on a regular basis, although one wonders how the Encyclopedia will cope with Catholicism questions after 1913!?

Catholic Scotland
www.catholic-scotland.org.uk
Jazzier in appearance than its neighbours south of the border, and featuring an irritating flashing banner promoting church candles and furniture, this is useful if you are seeking a link to one of Scotland's Catholic communities or parishes. They are featured on the entry page, which has a search engine for convenient location of specific material. The site is hosted by the Dunkeld News (a copy of which can be downloaded). Inside the site, some of the frames were difficult to negotiate. News updates are available by email subscription.

Desperate Preacher
www.desperatepreacher.com
Now priests lacking inspiration can go to the internet to solve their sermon-writing problems. This US-based resource contains quotes, prayers, and sermons broken down into categories, including jokes. Topics on the A-Z cover traditional themes, ranging from Advent to Worship. Judging by the number of hits, there are priests out there making substantial use of this site. No membership necessary, although membership is available for extra benefits. Related materials can also be purchased via Amazon.com

Jesuits in Britain
www.jesuit.ie/uk/ohome/frames.html
This is an accessible site, containing areas on prayer, reflecting faith, and history. Links to the worldwide organisation were down at the time of research.

Latin American Catholicism
www.acusd.edu/theo/ref-latino.html
This is a useful link page of documentation, primarily of an academic nature, to English, Spanish and Portuguese language sites.

orthodox christianity

Defining 'orthodox Christianity' is problematic. The term here primarily applies to beliefs that describe themselves as 'orthodox'.

www.coptic.net/
The Christian Coptic Orthodox Church Of Egypt

Overall rating: ★ ★ ★ ★ ★			
Classification:	Information	**Readability:**	★ ★ ★
Updating:	Regularly	**Reliability:**	★ ★ ★ ★
Navigation:	★ ★ ★	**Speed:**	★ ★ ★ ★

US

This is an authoritative and effective introduction to the fascinating world of Coptic Christianity, which is based in Egypt, but is networked throughout the world (especially via the web).

SPECIAL FEATURES

The Entry Page is hyperlinked to a wealth of rich images detailing many aspects of the faith, illustrated with images and sound files (all accessible from the main text). You might want to print the main text out, and take it away for a read, before venturing into the hyperlinked sections. Chanting, tapestry, iconography and music are just some of the sections on this regularly updated site, which is an excellent gateway worthy of repeated visits.

OTHER FEATURES

Coptic Search Engine is a neat interface to hundreds of Coptic-related pages. The engine is located in the site map, which also lists over 100 other Coptic sites.

+++ <_Click here for Coptic Network Archives_> >+++

The Christian Coptic Orthodox Church Of Egypt

The site is a perfect introduction to Coptic Christianity, worthy of repeated visits, providing a real insight into faith and practice.

www.nireland.com/orthodox/celtic.htm
Celtic Orthodox Christianity Homepage

Overall rating: ★ ★ ★ ★			
Classification:	Encyclopedia	**Readability:**	★ ★ ★
Updating:	Regularly	**Reliability:**	★ ★ ★
Navigation:	★ ★ ★ ★	**Speed:**	★ ★ ★ ★ ★

UK

The history, faith and life of the ancient churches of the British Isles have become a popular area of interest. The site is easy to navigate, and its material is clear and authoritative.

SPECIAL FEATURE

Saints is a substantial area of the site, listing more than 30 lives, ten selections of saints' writings, and 40 ikons (from Saint Aidan of Lindisfarne to Saint Nectan the Martyr).

OTHER FEATURES

This site focuses on the study of Celtic and Old English Christianity, and links into resources on Celtic and Old English worship, Celtic and Old English saints, and book and ikon sources.

There's plenty to interest the non-committed general reader, as well as those seeking to develop their expertise in ancient Christianity from an orthodox perspective.

www.goarch.org/
Greek Orthodox Diocese of America

Overall rating: ★ ★ ★			
Classification:	Information	Readability:	★ ★ ★
Updating:	Regularly	Reliability:	★ ★ ★
Navigation:	★ ★ ★	Speed:	★ ★ ★ ★

GR US

The Greek Orthodox Diocese of America has produced a well-organised high-tech site, which features among its services a scrolling news service, saints' days, an online store, and electronic greetings cards.

SPECIAL FEATURES

Multimedia is impressive: audio files of live Byzantine music and Greek broadcasts, church services, and a choice of videos in Greek and English (History of the Byzantine Empire, Archbishop Spyridon speaking on a variety of issues and Ecumenical Patriarch Bartholomew delivering his Easter Message). You can also take a QuickTime Virtual Reality tour of Constantinople.

OTHER FEATURES

Links lists Greek Orthodox monasteries throughout the world, although in many cases the URLs take you to academic pages of information (produced in Greece and elsewhere) rather than directly to the monastery.

Greek Orthodox institutions throughout the world are linked into this site, making it a great starting point to explore faith and practices.

www.russian-orthodox-church.org.ru/en.htm
Russian Orthodox Church

Overall rating: ★ ★ ★			
Classification:	Information	Readability:	★ ★
Updating:	Regularly	Reliability:	★ ★ ★
Navigation:	★ ★ ★	Speed:	★ ★ ★

RU

Navigation has been much improved on these pages, belonging to the Russian Orthodox Patriarchate of Moscow His Holiness Patriarch Alexy II, whose photo graces the entry page. The green sidebar to the left takes you to all the relevant content.

SPECIAL FEATURE

Church News is laced with Russian political perspectives, news, photos, and speeches. Detailed information relating to Church activities and personnel (including appointments) is provided in the pages, which provide the Patriarchal view on world affairs and inter-faith dialogues.

OTHER FEATURES

The Patriarch's pronouncements are given prominence on the front page – but took ages to download. The Historical Background section is sparse, and the Orthodox Resources pages were under construction.

Direct from the Patriarch's office, this official site tells you a great deal about contemporary Russian faith, and the political influence of the Church in the post-glasnost era.

OTHER ORTHODOX SITES

Coptic Liturgy
http://pharos.bu.edu/cn/collections/AudioCopticLiturgies/
The Holy Coptic Orthodox Liturgy, according to St. Gregory, can be heard via an MP3 player from Melbourne, Australia. Ignore the introduction (unless you are an Arabic speaker and go to the Intercession and Gregorian Litanies (about 10800k in size) for a sample of the beautiful sounds of Coptic faith.

Cyberdesert
http://users.otenet.gr/~marinarb/
Orthodox saints and works are indexed, and select resources provided.

Orthodox Christian Resources on the Internet
www.hrweb.org/orthodox/
This is a thorough site, containing liturgies, bibles, prayers, and calendars – materials for orthodox believers and newcomers to the religion.

The Orthodox Church of Antioch in Great Britain
www.antiochian-orthodox.co.uk/indexnj.html
Find out about activities in the Deanery, read sermons from various priests (some of whom actively participate in this site's construction), and learn of activities throughout Britain (including the construction of new communities and buildings). This contains a useful concise introduction to orthodox beliefs, and resources for prayer and contemplation.

The Saints of the Orthodox Church
www.goarch.org/access/Companion_to_Orthodox_Church/Saints.html

Richly illustrated pages, including extensive listing of saints' writings, and study resources.

Other Christian Paths

There's a wealth of Christianity out there on the internet. The following is a choice selection, representing some of the diversity of Christian faith and expression throughout the world.

Amish and Mennonites
Remember the 1985 Oscar-winning film 'Witness', starring Harrison Ford? That was set in an Amish community, and revealed to the wider world the hidden lifestyle of this Anabaptist group (linked to the Mennonites). The internet sheds further light on them.

www.amish-heartland.com			
Amish Heartland			
Overall rating: ★ ★ ★			
Classification:	Information	Readability:	★ ★ ★
Updating:	Regularly	Reliability:	★ ★ ★
Navigation:	★ ★ ★	Speed:	★ ★ ★ ★
UK			

Although Pennsylvania is the primary location of Amish people, Ohio also has an Amish community, which this site focuses on.

SPECIAL FEATURES

Frequently Asked Questions offers revealing insight into the lifestyle of the Amish. Questions that caught our attention included: 'Why is it that Amish cannot own or drive cars, but they can ride in them?' (Amish accept a ride when necessary.) 'Why don't the Amish use electricity?' (To separate from the world and be self-sufficient.) 'Why don't the Amish want to have their pictures taken?' (Photos are 'graven images'.) If they don't use electricity, how can the Amish sometimes have water heaters, stoves and refrigerators in their homes? (They use natural gas.)

Amish Shopping Mall is the site's affiliated online shop, selling authentic products produced by Ohio's Amish craftspeople. Whether the Amish foods would travel is open to question, but their books, hand-made quilts and baby gifts look like attractive products. Products are priced in US dollars. While American customers can purchase items via a secure server with credit cards, international customers have to email their enquiry or telephone the shop directly.

OTHER FEATURES

Amish Heartland contains various articles on the Amish, linked to a subscription magazine. Despite the Amish reluctance for being photographed, there is a photo library on the site.

Forget Harrison Ford, and you can learn a great deal about Amish faith from this site.

OTHER AMISH AND MENNONITE SITES

Mennonite Connections on the World Wide Web
www-personal.umich.edu/~bpl/mennocon.html
For those seeking greater depth of information about Mennonites and Amish peoples, this page links to all aspects of beliefs, including theology, history, and resources. There are hundreds of links, although little in the way of explanation. The site author, Bradley Lehman, states that it contains every page on the Mennonites he has heard of (we counted more than 300).

Ask the Amish
www.800padutch.com/askamish.html
'Ask the Amish' allows you to post your questions, although the archive of FAQs might pre-empt you. Several questions were based on the observations of people visiting Amish sites, and focused in particular on Amish lifestyles.

Third Way Café
www.thirdway.com
Third Way Café is produced by Mennonite Media, in order to explain the belief structure of the Mennonite Churches of the US and Canada. The Café links to related media, and statements on Mennonite perspectives relating to religious and social issues. You can also receive an email newsletter by subscription.

Lehman's Non Electric Catalogue
www.lehmans.com
The Amish sustain a self-sufficient lifestyle, and don't use electricity. Where do they buy their goods? This catalogue shows some of the products the Amish use, in order to fulfill their objectives: 'Hand-powered kitchen appliances, homesteading tools, grain mills, cheese-making supplies, composting toilets, oil lamps and gas lights, water pumps and filters, gas refrigerators, wood-burning stoves, and much more. Many of the items date to the 1800s.'

Assyrian Church of the East

www.cired.org/ace.html
Holy Apostolic Catholic Assyrian Church of the East: the E-Messenger

Overall rating: ★ ★ ★ ★			
Classification:	Information	Readability:	★ ★ ★ ★ ★
Updating:	Regularly	Reliability:	★ ★ ★ ★
Navigation:	★ ★ ★	Speed:	★ ★ ★ ★ ★

US

'The Church of the East has a sacramental system which resembles the sacramental systems of the Greek and Latin traditions' and the fascinating history is detailed on this site. Navigate via the front page, which lists all areas: don't be dissuaded from exploring when the English buttons transform into Syriac (links go to English pages). Areas of the site require Shockwave, RealPlayer and Adobe Acrobat.

SPECIAL FEATURES

Church Liturgy and Calendar presents the Eucharist Liturgy of the Church of the East , as celebrated in Edessan Classical Syriac.

Syriac Documents includes the Lord's Prayer in Syriac. Articles on Theology and Sacraments outlines the main areas of belief, including festivals and ritualistic practices. About Assyrian Church of the East explains the church's history, and relations with the Roman Catholic Church.

The Assyrian diaspora makes good use of the internet elsewhere, and that knowledge has been incorporated into these pages.

Branch Davidians

http://start.at/mt.carmel/
Mt Carmel – Branch Davidian website

Overall rating: ★ ★			
Classification:	Information	Readability:	★
Updating:	Regularly	Reliability:	★ ★
Navigation:	★ ★	Speed:	★ ★ ★

US

While associated in the contemporary context with David Koresh, the Branch Davidians have their roots in a divergence from the Seventh Day Adventists, founded in 1929 by Victor Houteff (1885-1955), who applied biblical exegesis to determine that he was an instrument of God. The Branch Davidians are one of several further cleavages from a Seventh Day Adventist schism. Events surrounding the bloody siege in Waco, Texas, in which federal officials killed Koresh and a number of his followers, have led to numerous conspiracy theories. Such theories have wide currency in different interest areas of the worldwide web, and are not necessarily linked to religious interests.

There's a bizarre mix of religion and Pokémon on the front page of this site. Ignoring the bouncing graphic, the page is headed by a photo of David Koresh, and links into discussions by and about Koresh, of which some of the authors are incarcerated in a US Penitentiary. The focus of the site is on the survivors of the siege, and its repercussions. The table of contents is hyperlinked inside the site, at the bottom of the visitors' page, and should lead to the elements of the pages concerning faith. However, the design of the site leaves much to be desired, including blue font on a dark cloud background. Trial transcripts includes more than 4,000 pages of content, in zip format, and is unsuitable for all but the most dedicated of surfers.

Although their representation and use of the internet is significant, the motives of the Branch Davidians in terms of faith remain obscure after visiting this site.

OTHER BRANCH DAVIDIAN SITES

The David Koresh Manuscript: Exposition Of The Seven Seals
www.everett.com/users/rorrim/manuscript.htm
This site contains biblical commentary and exegesis from David Koresh's manuscripts, some of which he was completing during the Waco siege. A proportion of this material was assembled from draft documents, and material rescued on computer disk from the site of the siege. This provides an insight into his apocalyptic worldview, and Koresh's analysis of his own prophetic status.

Rebuild the Church
www.wizardsofaz.com/waco/waco5a.html
Texas talk-show host Alex Jones established this site to challenge the assumptions surrounding events at Waco, and directly confront what he deemed to be the heavy-handed actions of the government against David Koresh. He seeks to rebuild the Davidian's church as 'a monument to freedom of religious and cultural expression, and as a reminder to the dangers of the government having police powers that are too wide and undefined'. You can make up your own mind on this campaigning site, which contains photographs of the rebuilding programme, and an opportunity for you to donate to the cause.

Church of Jesus Christ of Latter Day Saints/ Mormons

www.lds.org/
Church of Jesus Christ of Latter Day Saints

Overall rating: ★ ★ ★ ★ ★			
Classification:	Information	**Readability:**	★ ★ ★ ★
Updating:	Daily	**Reliability:**	★ ★ ★ ★
Navigation:	★ ★ ★ ★	**Speed:**	★ ★ ★ ★ ★

US

This is the official Mormon church internet site, in 34 languages, detailing Mormon beliefs and practices. The front page has a magazine format, with central zones listed on the left-hand sidebar, and current events on the right-hand sidebar. Given the wealth of pages on the site, the effective search engine and site map, available on the top right of the front page, are particularly useful.

SPECIAL FEATURES

Basic Beliefs offers a succinct introduction to the church, including founder Joseph Smith's personal account of his visions. The church can be emailed for a free copy of the Book of Mormon, although this may come with two Elders attached to spread the word in person.

The Scriptures presents searchable versions of the Old and New Testaments (King James Version), together with the Book of Mormon, described as 'another testament of Jesus Christ'. The summaries of the book's chapters offer a useful introduction to the faith, and may direct surfers to areas of interest. The Scriptures section offers study aids, background information, and notation of source materials.

Family History introduces the substantial amount of information on family history research, which is a central

feature of Mormon practices, linking into the church's Family History Department archive of 285 million deceased persons. A related page allows surfers to search for individual names within the archive (www.familysearch.org).

OTHER FEATURES

Audio Scriptures allows you to listen to a choice of RealPlayer or Windows Media versions of the scriptures, which download quickly. Each page comes with a text accompaniment. The narrators come straight out of Hollywood, complete with divine echo.

Along with other forms of media, the Mormon church has been making effective use of the internet for several years, providing useful material for the curious as well as the international Mormon community.

OTHER MORMON SITES

All About Mormons

www.mormons.org/

This is not an official site, but attempts to express mainstream church beliefs. There are over 2,000 pages about the church, and the site makes the claim that it is 'the internet's largest and most comprehensive source of accurate information about the Church'.

Mormon Origins

www.xmission.com/~research/about/index.htm

Mormon Origins incorporates historical and academic data relating to the Church of Jesus Christ of Latter Day Saints, and founder Joseph Smith's teachings. Archives include genealogy on the Smith family, historical documentation (such as Joseph Smith Junior's first recorded Revelation in 1828), and copies of Smith's journals.

Book of Mormon Answerman

www.new-jerusalem.com/bom-answerman/

Submit a question to Answerman on the Book of Mormon, or search for an answer in the site's archive.

The Utah Baby Namer

www.geocities.com/Heartland/3450/

'An online help for parents looking for that distinctive name that says "I'm a Utah Mormon!" '.

First Church of Cyberspace

www.godweb.org/index1.html		
First Church of Cyberspace		
Overall rating: ★ ★ ★		
Classification: Information	**Readability:**	★ ★ ★
Updating: Regularly	**Reliability:**	★ ★ ★
Navigation: ★ ★	**Speed:**	★ ★ ★ ★
US		

Created by Presbyterian minister Charles Henderson, this makes good use of web technology in well-presented pages and features. The Church claims to be the first to organise itself within cyberspace, 'dropping clues that point to the presence of the Creator within the creative chaos of the internet'. The site itself is somewhat chaotic to navigate: scrolling down the index page is probably the least painful option.

SPECIAL FEATURES

Sanctuary and Prayer sections were particularly thoughtful, incorporating reproductions of classic art, and music. The religious nature of the internet is discussed, including Java technology, the connection between sacred text and hypertext, and a Blinking Psalm applet.

OTHER FEATURES

A spoof Church of Cyberspace-Microsoft merger was 'highlighted'. Henderson links to material he has written for About.com on Christianity, and Christianity and Sexuality.

The First Church of Cyberspace's content is innovative, and rich in detail, although difficult to travel around at times.

Free Church of Scotland

www.freechurch.org		
Free Church of Scotland		
Overall rating: ★ ★ ★		
Classification: Information	**Readability:**	★ ★ ★
Updating: Regularly	**Reliability:**	★ ★ ★
Navigation: ★ ★ ★	**Speed:**	★ ★ ★ ★
UK		

The Free Church of Scotland have produced a well-designed site, explaining the essential basis of its faith, and outlining its role as the 'official' church in the light of a split in January 2000. 'It continues to preach the Gospel, dedicated to an inspired and infallible Bible, the doctrine contained in the Westminster Confession of Faith, and the Regulative principle of worship, by which the Free Church employs unaccompanied psalm-singing in her worship, along with prayer and the preaching of the Word.' The Free Church has a wide, and often isolated, group of adherents (for example, those in the Scottish Highlands and Islands). The internet is ideal for presenting contemporary news and religious material to those who are wired into the net. It has been promoted and utilised by educational authorities in the region.

SPECIAL FEATURE

Sing Psalms is probably the most interesting section to neutral surfers. Calum Martin, a music teacher and deacon from the island of Lewis, designed it: 'During the course of his work he uses a score-writing programme called Sibelius, and it occurred to him that this would be a great way to promote the Psalms on the site, especially to the non-music readers, if they could hear what they sounded like and learn them by ear.' There is a link to the free download of Sibelius, which only takes a few minutes to install (3.2MB in size plus manual, for Mac or Windows). A download of Scorch, a program to read scores on the internet, is also required (900k). At the time of browsing, 27 psalms were available to experiment with. Titles included Tallis's Canon, Bays of Harris, and Angels Song. This worked well, in providing the musical notation to various psalms, which the Free Church member could learn in order to sing psalms unaccompanied in services.

OTHER FEATURES

The remainder of the site includes articles in Gaelic, a detailed library of historical documentation, a children's section, and a list of churches and congregations in Scotland and elsewhere.

This should hit the right note for church musicians, and should be commended for its innovative content.

Jehovah's Witnesses

www.watchtower.org
Watchtower

Overall rating: ★ ★ ★ ★			
Classification:	Information	Readability:	★ ★ ★ ★
Updating:	Regularly	Reliability:	★ ★ ★
Navigation:	★ ★ ★ ★	Speed:	★ ★ ★ ★ ★

US

This is a well-organised 'official' site, making good use of graphics, and containing a wealth of information and articles about the Jehovah's Witnesses in 20 languages. As well as tracts and publications, there are sections containing medical information and advice relating to Witnesses' beliefs (such as bloodless surgery), and a substantial archive on other medical issues. The front page highlights current articles, and the site can be navigated via the ten buttons on the right-hand side. The content is consistent and clear, with individual pages navigable via the links on the top of the page.

SPECIAL FEATURES

Beliefs and Activities presents online versions of brochures and articles, explaining the background and faith of Jehovah's Witnesses. 'What Does God Require of Us?' is an introductory biblical study course, which can be navigated via the subject headings on the left of the page. Each page has a printable version.

Medical introduces the Witnesses' perspective on medical treatment, including their controversial opinions on 'non-blood treatment'. There are also some interesting general articles on children with learning disabilities, lifestyle, and quitting smoking.

The magazine format offers an easy entry point to the Witnesses' worldview, although if you send them your address you can expect a knock on the door.

OTHER JEHOVAH WITNESSES SITES

Jehovah's Witnesses United
http://jehovah.to/

This provides an alternative perspective, along with interesting resources on issues including the Nazi persecution of Witnesses, biblical exegesis, and religious freedom. The news headlines are regularly updated with stories about the Jehovah's Witnesses. This site is central to the Jehovah's Witnesses' webring, which links to many other sites.

www.jesus.org.uk/
Jesus Army

Overall rating: ★ ★ ★ ★			
Classification: Information		**Readability:**	★ ★ ★ ★
Updating: Regularly		**Reliability:**	★ ★ ★ ★
Navigation: ★ ★ ★ ★		**Speed:**	★ ★ ★ ★ ★

UK

The Jesus Army provides a lively UK site, which clearly explains their evangelical faith perspective as a 'church without prejudice'. Key areas can be located via the icons, which also highlight links on the menu to areas such as the Magazine and Jesus Explosion. There is a strong interactive element on the site, with a chat room and an online forum.

SPECIAL FEATURES

Magazine is a street newspaper with provocative articles, such as 'Thai Sex Romp Haunts Krishna Man' (about a convert to Jesus Army), and 'Mobbed By Wild Teens! Jesus Joy Calms Hostile Crowd'.

Extra! includes a section entitled Can We Help You, an email prayer service, which notes: 'Sorry, we can only respond to personal requests. No prayer spamming, please!'

OTHER FEATURES

There's a Jesus Army shop where 'Witnesswear' can be purchased, together with books, music and videos. Music can be previewed using a RealPlayer or MP3.

Jesus Army present an overwhelming sense of energetic enthusiasm, combined with strong design features, although their trendiness may not appeal to more sedate surfers.

Seventh Day Adventist

www.vop.com
Voice of Prophecy

Overall rating: ★ ★ ★			
Classification:	Information	Readability:	★ ★ ★
Updating:	Daily	Reliability:	★ ★
Navigation:	★ ★ ★ ★	Speed:	★ ★ ★

US

Established as a radio station in 1929, the Voice of Prophecy now makes great use of the web to broadcast sermons and other material (using RealPlayer). Transcripts of talks are available. The left-hand side bar links to all the zones in the site, and the style is consistent.

SPECIAL FEATURES

Bible Guide offers an online study course, complete with certificate for successful completion. No registration is necessary to take the first lesson, which has an interactive element with its question and answer form at the end of the lesson: 'The universe resulted from an accidental explosion. True or False?'

Prayer Request enables surfers to submit a prayer by email, which will be integrated into a special weekly prayer circle.

OTHER FEATURES

Children's Stories contains more than 50 RealPlayer files, covering many sections from the Old Testament.

Voice of Prophecy is a slick example of online evangelism, but is probably of greatest appeal to existing believers.

Unification Church

http://unification.net/
Unification Church

Overall rating: ★ ★			
Classification:	Information	Readability:	★
Updating:	Regularly	Reliability:	★ ★
Navigation:	★	Speed:	★ ★ ★ ★

US

This text-heavy site has content in more than 20 languages, providing perspectives on the Unification Church, and detailing pronouncements of Rev. Sun Myung Moon and Mrs. Hak Ja Han Moon (the True Parents), whose activities have included interpreting biblical texts. The page contains substantial hyperlinks, many of which are primarily aimed at those with existing knowledge of the Church. FAQs lists 50 volumes of questions and speeches from Moon date back to 1956.

SPECIAL FEATURES

Teachings are archived, including Family Pledge, True Parents and the Completed Testament Age, and the View of the Principle of the Providential History of Salvation. Includes the history of Sun Myung Moon, from his North Korean origins, through to the global religious movement of today.

Comprehensive but not accessible to newcomers, lacking guidance or navigation aids.

Universal Life Church

http://ulc.org/ulchq/index.htm			
Universal Life Church			
Overall rating: ★ ★ ★ ★			
Classification: Information		**Readability:**	★ ★ ★ ★
Updating: Regularly		**Reliability:**	★ ★ ★
Navigation: ★ ★ ★		**Speed:**	★ ★ ★ ★ ★
US			

The Universal Life Church believes everyone is already a member of their church and can be a minister, and as such offers ordinations online. It was founded by Kirby J Hensley, and offers online absolution, ordination, and a chance for individuals to establish their own ministries. The site is navigated via the purple side bar, directing the pious to various zones of interest.

SPECIAL FEATURES

Absolution incorporates plenary indulgence by email, with a printable certificate to prove forgiveness.

Be Ordained is certainly inclusive, with RealPlayer introduction, a section for the hearing impaired (using video), and a special link for AOL users. You can choose to be ordained in black and white or colour, depending on your printer. Be aware that your email and personal details will be entered onto the Church's database.

ULC Online Chapel is for those seeking to learn more about the Church, through RealPlayer broadcasts of Brother Daniel's sermons, and the promise of live radio and chat.

OTHER FEATURES

Bookstore offers a broad selection of titles from diverse faith perspectives, which can be ordered through Amazon.com. News was quaint, describing the disquiet of one member towards the thousands of new ministers recruited via the internet, and presents the Church's views on religious freedom of expression.

The Church is sincere in its beliefs, and is certainly jumping over conventional boundaries while promoting its opinion that 'the fewer beliefs one has the better for the individual'.

OTHER CHRISTIAN SITES

Baptist Union of Great Britain
www.baptist.org.uk

The Baptist Union of Great Britain's website took some time to download and use. The white font on a sky blue background with grey 'watermark' takes some getting used to, distracting the reader from such subjects as 'Who'd be a Baptist?' and 'Baptist Roots'. The level of information is basic and introductory in nature, although there is little in the way of direct 'religious content', apart from a Thought for the Week. The listing of resources includes free print materials, available by mail order, together with other publications.

Bible Gateway
http://bible.gospelcom.net/

This is a Bible search engine resource in ten languages, facilitating keyword and subject searches. It draws on several versions of English language Bible translations, including the King James Revised Standard Version, New American Standard Bible, and the New International Version. More resources are being added regularly.

Christian Classics Ethereal Library
http://ccel.wheaton.edu/
From St. Alphonsus to John Wesley, and points in between, the Library is comprehensive, exhaustive, and full of substantial resources that you can download. It probably helps if you know what you are looking for, in order not to be overwhelmed by the sheer breadth of links. Famous names include St. Thomas Aquinas, St. Augustine, and Martin Luther; also writers such as John Donne, John Bunyan, and Lev Nikolayevich Tolstoy. It may be easier to read the books, rather than the screen!

Christian Music
http://music.crosswalk.com/
Christian music is big business in the United States. Witness Crosswalk, containing nine purchasing options for CDs, conversations with musicians, and free music downloads, includes links to live broadcasts of Christian radio stations and videos.

Christian Mystics and Their Writings
www.digiserve.com/mystic/external_links/Christian/mystics.html
This is a one-stop shop for Christian mysticism, containing links to libraries, extensive biographical data, and significant writings from a variety of sources and religious perspectives. (See full site review in Esoteric section, p.106.)

Church of the Brethren Network
www.cob-net.org/inform.htm
The Church of the Brethren Network includes a timeline, charting the development of the Brethren back to the 15th century. Among literature on the Church and its activities, the site includes a substantial prayer section.

Church of the Open Mind (Unitarian Church)
www.hibbert.org.uk/
The Unitarian Church represents a 'liberal' perspective on Christian beliefs, and this is reflected in pages on social responsibility, the history of the church, and guidelines to worship. The Cybersermons feature is text based and limited to three lectures articulating Unitarian belief frameworks.

Elim Pentecostal Church Web Site
www.elim.org.uk
'The Elim Pentecostal Church was founded in 1915 by a Welshman in Monaghan, Ireland. George Jeffreys was an outstanding evangelist and church planter. He had a Welsh Congregational background, was strongly influenced by the Welsh Revival of 1904, and was introduced to Pentecost by an Anglican vicar, Rev Alexander Boddy of Sunderland.' The Elim Church history is detailed here on a well-designed site, and their evangelism programme detailed in full (although not updated for at least a year, at the time of visiting). The Elim seem well wired, with a listing of more than 40 local Pentecostal churches with websites.

Goshen
www.goshen.net/
Search the net in 'safety' with this Christian search engine. Also links to various evangelical resources, associated with the Crosswalk.com site.

Hildegard of Bingen
www.healingchants.com/hvb_links.html
Discover the intuitive writings of Hildegard of Bingen (1098-1179); her chants are presented in Latin and English, there are links to audio files containing her music, and the original score can be viewed.

Jesus People USA
www.jpusa.org/
'We believe that the Bible is the uniquely inspired and inerrant Word of God and is fully binding on all matters of faith, doctrine, and practice'. Ministries (and related businesses, including music groups, online stores and festivals), and participation opportunities are incorporated into this site, which highlights the organisation's social

programmes. Jesus People have outreach activities relating to urban ministry, including pregnancy counselling, homeless shelters, and teaching programmes.

Methodist Motorsports Evangelism
www.wnccumc.org/docs/methmotorsports.htm
This website publicises an outreach programme on the racetrack, based in North Carolina: 'Pastor H.R. (Buddy) Compton, a racing enthusiast, had been looking for some time to have a Methodist presence at the race track. "Our purpose is simple – to spread the good news of God's love at the race track," says Compton. "Racing is the number one spectator sport in the country, and United Methodists have a tradition of 'going where the people are."' Only in America.

Original Province of the Anglican Catholic Church
www.anglicancatholic.org/
The Original Province of the Anglican Catholic Church (ACC) is based in the United States, with dioceses in India, the UK, Australasia and South Africa (all with websites). The historical pages explain the rationale for the ACC: 'That we can say what the ACC is and believes, and that what she is and believes leads back to the central tradition of Christendom represented by the Eastern Orthodox and the ancient Councils, is our chief justification.' It discusses the use of various liturgical sources within its practices, and the sermons are regularly updated (text versions only).

Presbyterian Church of Wales
www.ebcpcw.org.uk/html/Eng/pcwintro.htm
Welsh and English language materials, including the history of the church, educational links, a confession of faith, and a link to download the church's newsletter.

Presbyterian Church, USA
http://horeb.pcusa.org/search/dailyreadings.htm
Daily readings are incorporated into this site, taken from the New Revised Standard Version of the Bible. The Catechism is also explained.

Protestant Hour
www.protestanthour.com/
The Protestant Hour has been running since 1945, as an ecumenical radio programme produced for an Episcopal Church, Evangelical Lutheran, Presbyterian, and United Methodist audience. It now broadcasts on the web, presenting an archive of sermons in RealAudio format, together with transcripts.

Reformed Evangelical Christians
www.grace.org.uk/faith/index.html
As well as listing the 'Five Points' or 'Doctrines of Grace' associated with Reformed Evangelical Christian identity, this site has links to other documentation, including Ancient Creeds and Historic Reformed Confessions (available to unzip). There is a clickable map of British Reformed Evangelical Christian churches, and contact details, networking these Christians together on the net.

Salvation Army – United Kingdom Territory
www.salvationarmy.org.uk/
'You don't have to wear a funny hat and blow a bugle. Not unless you're a Salvationist – and not even then'. This is a professional, information-rich website, linked to the Army's international pages. The history pages provide effective summaries on the Army's founder William Booth and his wife Catherine, together with the origins of the Army's uniform. Religious content includes Words of Life, 'weekly, bite-sized Bible readings, written to bring readers closer to God through prayer and praise...'. The Salvation Army's publications, including the famous 'War Cry', have electronic editions available online.

Shaker Manuscripts
www.passtheword.org/shaker-manuscripts/
The introduction is intriguing, and compels the curious to explore the site in more detail: 'Here you may be troubled by what you find; here the foundation of your religious life may literally be shaken – as only the early Shakers knew how to

do ... but then again, you may be awakened, challenged, inspired, mentored and nurtured by what they have preserved for us... and here you may even find a confirmation of some truths that you have known in your heart of hearts ... all along'. There's a wealth of religious information here, including Divine Book of Holy and Eternal Wisdom, but no obvious signs of furniture.

The Christ Path
www.christpath.com
'The Ezine of Christian Mystics – Traditional and Contemporary.' Regularly updated with articles and information – including a Quote of the Day (with commentary).

The Gnostic Society Library
www.webcom.com/~gnosis/gnostsoc.html
This is an extensive collection of RealAudio lectures from the Gnostic Society of Los Angeles, which the surfer can download and listen to at leisure. There are some interesting titles here, on a broad range of subjects, including: An Introduction to Kabbalah and The Zohar, God, The Shadow and Dr. Jung, JRR Tolkien's The Lord of the Rings: Gnosis for Our Day, and The Sorrow of Sophia: Feminine Divine Image of Suffering. Cassette versions of these lectures can be ordered online.

The Holy Island of Lindisfarne
www.lindisfarne.org.uk/
The site incorporates information on the churches and retreats contained on the Holy Island, including lives of St. Cuthbert and St. Aidain, and historical background material. Tide tables are contained on the site, for the safety of visitors.

The Religious Society of Friends
www.quaker.org/
This is a comprehensive link page to Quaker-related sites, and is not without a sense of humour. It contained introductory information on the Society's 'practices', presented without frames or images, naturally. We liked the links to sites that use the 'Quaker' name, but are totally unrelated to the Religious Society of Friends (i.e. Quaker Parrots, Quaker Chemical and Broglio's Quaker Stout). The site also has a section on Quaker Oats, and 'Quaker-named sites without a clue'.

The United Pentecostal Church International
www.upci.org/
The United Pentecostal Church International focuses on a United States audience, but has some content of general interest. Click on the links to Harvestime broadcasts and you'll find an archive of weekly sermons dating back to 1998. These RealPlayer recordings certainly give a flavour of the Pentecostal experience, with titles such as 'Jesus is Really Coming', 'What is There in Religion?' and 'Blood Stained Pages'. Elsewhere on the site, prayer requests can be submitted by email and shared with various prayer groups. Our prayer would be to stop irritating boxes appearing on otherwise serviceable websites, as this site seems to demand a Macromedia Shockplayer 8, and persistently produces download windows if you don't have one, and don't want one! You can also find an Apostolic pen pal, via the site's extensive database, although they state categorically that this 'IS NOT (their emphasis) for finding new partners, boyfriends, girlfriends, or spouses'.

hinduism

There is a substantial amount of Hindu-related material available on the internet. Many of the Hinduism sites available online are high-tech, in part reflecting the fact that India has a thriving computer software industry. There is also considerable duplication of resources, and a large number of GIF-heavy homepages. It is definitely one of the areas on faith on the web in which a series of selected links is useful.

www.channel4.co.uk/kumbhmela/
Kumbh Mela – Channel Four Television

Overall rating: ★ ★ ★ ★ ★			
Classification:	Information	Readability:	★ ★ ★ ★
Updating:	Seasonal	Reliability:	★ ★ ★ ★ ★
Navigation:	★ ★ ★ ★	Speed:	★ ★ ★ ★

UK

In 2001, over thirty million pilgrims took part in the auspicious Kumbh Mela religious festival, at the confluence of the rivers known as Sangam at Allahabad, India. Bathing here accelerates progress to nirvana, absolves sin and ends the reincarnation cycle. The next Kumbh Mela will be in 2013, but in the interim there are websites providing fascinating information, photographs and film material of the event. This state-of-the-art site is one of the most interesting, featuring video-clips and the 'real stories' of selected participants: Channel 4 sent a film crew to chronicle the 2001 Kumbh Mela, and the 'key characters' and highlights were featured on a dedicated website. Requires RealPlayer, Flash player, and QuickTime.

SPECIAL FEATURES

Characters introduces six of the people followed by Channel 4's film crew, with brief biographies and a video introduction (requires RealPlayer). You can meet Kannai Das Baul, 'the most renowned wandering musical Sadhu' or holy man, who is devoted to the goddess of death, and spends a significant amount of time smoking marijuana. There is also a clip of the teenage Sadhu Hathi Giri, who underwent an initiation ceremony at the Kumbh (thankfully, we are spared the video film of the initiation – not for the squeamish!). Other pilgrims and sadhus provide rich insight into the lives of holy people and their role in Hindu culture.

Sadhu Wisdom requires the 'enlightenment' of a Flash player to use this page, which is fun. Six cartoon depictions of Sadhus are presented sitting in a holy circle of fire. Clicking the cursor within the circle reveals pearls of Sadhu wisdom, such as: 'When you are naked you can't hide anything, and before long you don't bother to try.'

OTHER FEATURES

Khumbarama provides panoramic shots of the festival, presenting selected scenes in 360 degrees. This requires QuickTime, and speakers if you are going to listen to the audio accompaniment. The entire festival was chronicled, and linked to specific film clips, detailing diverse aspects of the Mela and the lives of the pilgrims.

An entertaining and informative website on Hinduism, providing an invaluable digital resource on the Kumbh Mela.

www.hubcom.com/tantric/

Shiva Shakti Mandalam: Tantrik Home Page

Overall rating: ★ ★ ★ ★ ★			
Classification:	Information	**Readability:**	★ ★ ★ ★
Updating:	Regularly	**Reliability:**	★ ★ ★ ★ ★
Navigation:	★ ★ ★ ★	**Speed:**	★ ★ ★ ★

UK

Is tantric tradition all about sex? Not according to the authors of this detailed site. Learn about the tantra in its many forms, as the site provides a number of approaches towards the tradition. The front page links to all the main areas of the site, under headings including Nathas and Yoga, Tantrik Ritual, Tantrik Translations, and Sanskrit Texts. Some of the material has a controversial nature, or has 'secret' origins: 'Since this site first came online in 1996, we have had some criticism for revealing mantras and yantras which are supposed, according to the texts themselves, to be secret ... At the same time, it is as well to realise that most of this information here is available in Sanskrit and Hindi versions, whether in print or in libraries'.

SPECIAL FEATURES

Glossary is helpful to those new to tantric terminology. There is a clickable A-Z (Abhaya to Yuga) listing.

Tantrik Texts introduces the principal works.

Sexuality in Tantrik Tradition explores why the schools of tantra have become synonymous with sex.

Easy to navigate, Shiva Shakti Mandalam makes great use of the web as a teaching tool, offering access to unique and often difficult-to-locate materials. (Also see Religion, Gender and Sexuality section.)

www.hindu.dk

Hinduism and Daily Life

Overall rating: ★ ★ ★ ★			
Classification:	Information	**Readability:**	★ ★ ★ ★
Updating:	Never	**Reliability:**	★ ★ ★ ★
Navigation:	★ ★ ★	**Speed:**	★ ★

DEN

This is a gentle introduction to the basics of Hindu beliefs, based on material gathered by anthropologist Lars Kjaerholm in south India over a 30-year period. The site is an academic collaboration between a Danish museum and a university, but the material is user-friendly and easy to navigate. All pages link back to a site-map, on the lower left of the page, or via clicking the button on the top left of the page. The top bar on the pages can also be used for quick navigation to specific sections of interest. Occasionally, the GIFs take some time to download, but are worth the wait. There are some links to QuickTime Windows Media clips illustrating myths; unfortunately non-functional at the time of writing. Some of the 'further reading' requires an Acrobat Reader. The site material is also available in Danish and German versions.

The site is divided into three main sections: Daily Life and Hinduism, Aiyanar (a significant god in Tamil Nadu, South India), and the Aiyappan pilgrimage. The What is Hinduism? link on the right-hand side of the page offers a text-only summary, useful if you haven't read anything on the religion before.

SPECIAL FEATURES

Daily Life and Hinduism makes good use of original slides and captions, presenting different 'stories' relating to women, food, ritual, and texts. The Religion link focuses on

Daily Life and Hinduism

We are in the South East of India, in the state of Tamil Nadu. This is an area with very old traditions both in agriculture and religion. In this part of India Hinduism has been protected against the many invasions that throughout history have come through the Khyber Pass.

Food
This story shows how labour is divided according to sex. It also gives a presentation of the close relationship between work and Hinduism.

Women
In this story the focus is on the women. What are their roles in the practice of Hinduism? This is a part of Hinduism that is often forgotten, but here we show you a less known side of religious life.

Religion
The focus is still on the women. But in this story we see how women play a role as oracles possessed by gods. People come to the women for advise, carrying offerings.
In this story we also meet professional dancers performing ritual dancing.

Rituals
Some of the rituals take place outside of the family sphere. In this story we see a Brahmin Priest teaching his son Vedic recitation. We also see some temples from the region of Tamil Nadu, as well as some offerings to the God Aiyanar.

the role some women play as oracles possessed by gods, illustrated by photographs and captions. How do 'ordinary housewives' become possessed trance mediums for a village god? What is the significance of pongal, and why are men only spectators in these rituals? Click on the Forward button at the bottom of the page to advance to the next slide; photographs can be enlarged.

OTHER FEATURES

Aiyappan and the Pilgrimage to Sabari explain the fast-growing form of bhakti worship, drawing on photos taken in 1999 at 'the third-largest annual religious gathering of people in the world, after the Vatican and Mecca'.

This is a unique online resource on Hinduism, with many pages presented from a female perspective, offering an insight into the role of faith in everyday life in South India.

www.indiadivine.com/
India Divine

Overall rating: ★ ★ ★ ★			
Classification:	Information	**Readability:**	★ ★ ★ ★
Updating:	Regularly	**Reliability:**	★ ★ ★ ★ ★
Navigation:	★ ★ ★	**Speed:**	★ ★ ★ ★

(IND)

India Divine is an extremely comprehensive site, based on Vedic scripts (or Hindu scriptures) that claims its content is 'provided by practitioners who have dedicated their lives to these ancient mystical sciences'. Navigate through the front page, which has a magazine format highlighting new articles, with side bars featuring the principal zones of the site, and interactive options.

SPECIAL FEATURES

Holy Men of India: Sadhus, Nagas and Babas is an article by Dolf Hartsuiker, with some fantastic photographs. It's a shame they are only small images, although you could right-click on them to copy and enlarge them (for your personal use only).

Personal answers to questions about Hinduism can be obtained by emailing the site.

Mystical Experiences contains actual experiences of holy men, with eight tales in the archive, and plans for expansions.

OTHER FEATURES

There are substantial RealPlayer lectures on Hinduism (from introductory level upwards), together with prayers and music, and you can also read sections on Natural Healing, Meditation, Yoga, and Hindu Folklore. A free screensaver

displaying incarnations of Lord Vishnu (2.20 Mb in size) was offered when we visited the site, and there is an Amazon.com link to a fine selection of 25 Hindu titles.

India Divine is recommended for the adventurous, and those with some prior knowledge of Hinduism, and is commendable for its interactive facilities.

www.hinduweb.org
The Hindu Universe

Overall rating: ★ ★ ★			
Classification:	Portal	**Readability:**	★ ★ ★
Updating:	Regularly	**Reliability:**	★ ★ ★ ★
Navigation:	★ ★	**Speed:**	★ ★ ★

US

The Hindu Universe is the website for GHEN (Global Hindu Electronic Networks), which has been online since 1994. GHEN is one of the many projects undertaken by HSC (Hindu Students Council). It may not be the most attractive site on the web, with its profusion of banners and an intrusive advert that 'greets' you every time you go to the index. It is, however, worth persevering with as a useful gateway into diverse Hindu-related resources. The site is also a user-centred community, in which members post their own sites onto its web space. The juxtaposition of banners for military organisations and Pyroto Mountain computer games with the Rigveda, for example, take some getting used to (the banners change regularly, and provide income to maintain the site). Some of the community sites are still works in progress, a fact that is not noted on the entry page.

SPECIAL FEATURES

Hindu Universe Major Sections are listed in the lower right-hand side of the index page. These provide useful introductions to interpretations of Hinduism. The section on God in Hindu Dharma and Representation in Temples contains links to pages on deities, some of which are accompanied by substantial GIFs and audio files (requiring a Windows Media player). This jpeg-heavy set of pages provides a detailed explanation of Hindu deities, including FAQs such as Why Does Hinduism Portray God as a Woman? and Why Do Hindus Worship Many Gods? Other links explore Planet deities, Avatars, and forms of the divine in Hinduism. The site is profusely illustrated with pictures of various deities. You need patience to delve into these resources, which are not always logically listed, but there are interesting discoveries at every turn on these pages! The Introduction to Hindu Dharma includes introductory online books (in English), including 'What Every Hindu Ought to Know' (in 25 hyperlinked chapters) written by a Hindu monk. The Hindu Universe's resource centre features information on interfaith dialogue, gods, sages and gurus, dharma and philosophy, and Hindu scriptures. For light relief, there is a 10-volume Culture Course (linked under Major Sections).

OTHER FEATURES

The Hindu Universe has a wealth of other digital resources, including links to news coverage, email postcards, live chat, discussion forums, and matrimonial announcements. The site hosts a book and music store (in conjunction with Amazon.com) and 10Mb of space for the web, a page builder, and 10Mb of email space (yourname@hinduweb.org) are also offered.

If you ignore the irritating 'pop-up' advert, the Hindu Universe is a great place to start looking for information about Hinduism, although a significant proportion of the content is designed for those with existing knowledge of the belief(s).

www.ammachi.org/
Ammachi

Overall rating: ★ ★			
Classification:	Information	Readability:	★ ★ ★
Updating:	Regularly	Reliability:	★ ★ ★
Navigation:	★ ★	Speed:	★ ★ ★ ★

US

'Mata Amritanandamayi is an embodiment of unconditional love, devoted to the service of all humanity'. This site contains a wealth of information about the 'Mother' (b.1953) from Kerala in India. It discusses the growth of her Ashram, and the nature of her 'practical spiritual discipline'. Navigate using the menu on the left, which outlines the principal areas including Charity, Teachings, Media and a magazine.

SPECIAL FEATURES

Puja discusses this ritualised form of worship, with sections on astrology, karma, and an order form for obtaining a personal puja by email. The prasad (offerings) are sent in the post, and advanced ordering is required.

Audio/Visual contains a video library, with recordings of scriptural classes and Ammachi media coverage (requires RealPlayer or Windows Media). Music Library is a substantial archive of bhajans (devotional music). However, the site was incorrectly hyperlinked at the time of writing, and playing the music was impossible. There is an emailing list for news about Ammachi, and a link to a secure shopping site called Mothersbooks for books, recordings, and frankincense (among other items).

Ammachi loses an overall star for broken links, but nevertheless is an interesting introduction to the 'Mother'.

OTHER HINDU SITES

Art and Aums

www.himalayanacademy.com/art/aum/display.html

Art and Aums is part of a detailed listing of Hindu resources, produced in Hawaii(!). A unique aspect was the photographic Art and Aums collection, representing the sacred Hindu symbol through different artwork collected by site users.

Culture and Religion in Ubud

www.indo.com/geo/ubud/culture.html

Hinduism is not just about India. There are a number of sites from other geographical and cultural contexts, of which this is but one example. These pages detail aspects of Balinese Hinduism from a non-academic perspective, with sections on its religious-historical development. The site could do with some photos, but is full of useful knowledge, especially for those lucky people heading for Bali on holiday.

Spirituality, Yoga, Hinduism Page [screen grab]

www.geocities.com/RodeoDrive/1415/

This well-resourced site is profusely illustrated with GIFs of Hindu gods and goddesses. Entering the site, one is expected first to make an offering to Lord Ganesha, before scrolling down the page to locate texts, pictures and prayers. Click on the hands to enter the main site. The site author has produced personal prayers in the pages, as well as providing historical and religious background information. The site has been running since 1995, and continues to be updated.

islam

The diversity of Islam is well represented on the internet, with many different religious, cultural and political perspectives online. Islam is often divided into Sunni 'orthodoxy', Shia Islam, and Sufi mystical Islam. You can learn more about the different perspectives through visiting the sites listed below. They will demonstrate that these divisions are not clear-cut, and that there can be substantial common ground in the core-values of faith. The Islamic duty of propagating religion is evident in some of the content.

http://harf.com
Harf Information Technology

Overall rating: ★ ★ ★ ★			
Classification:	hformation	Readability:	★ ★ ★
Updating:	Regularly	Reliability:	★ ★ ★ ★ ★
Navigation:	★ ★ ★ ★	Speed:	★ ★ ★

EGY

This is an impressive multilingual site from Egypt, Sunni orthodox in orientation, containing many detailed pages on aspects of Islam. These are listed in the left-hand box, and include Qur'an, Islamic Dictionary, Al-Islam, and Hadith (sayings of the Prophet Muhammad). There are also free downloads of Islamic software, appropriate for determining the time and direction of prayer. Many of the products available online can also be purchased on CDRom through this site.

SPECIAL FEATURES

Qur'an is a comprehensive database about the Revelation. Click on the left-hand side bar box entitled Display: First

Surah. This presents an English translation of the meaning from the Arabic script (Arabic being deemed the purest form of the Revelation). The Arabic script is contained in the yellow box. At the bottom of the page, click on Recitation, and choose either Al-Husari or Al-Hudhafi to hear distinctive, high-quality recordings (using RealPlayer). If you want to hear more, select a Surah number in the top Java box on the page, or return to the Qur'an front page and choose a subject from the list, to hear relevant verses.

Islamic Dictionary is a searchable resource of significant terms in English and Arabic. The dictionary is searchable via the box on the left-hand side of the page, which has a drop-down menu also allowing searches of the Qur'an.

OTHER FEATURES

Clicking the Al-Islam link on the top left of each page can also access a substantial proportion of site content. Hajj outlines pilgrimage's historical and ritualistic significance in detail.

The Qur'an interface is first-class, and other areas of the site are easy to navigate, making this site a good resource on aspects of Islam.

www.islam.org/
IslamiCity

Overall rating: ★ ★ ★ ★ ★			
Classification:	Portal	**Readability:**	★ ★ ★ ★
Updating:	Regularly	**Reliability:**	★ ★ ★ ★
Navigation:	★ ★ ★ ★	**Speed:**	★ ★ ★

US 🛈

IslamiCity is a superbly organised resource, which represents a great starting point to exploring the Muslim faith on the internet, containing hundreds of pages of content presented from a Sunni perspective. The entry page clearly indicates the central areas of the site, hyperlinked under the IslamiCity logo. The left-hand side bar contains links to Community, Portal, Devotion and Commerce sections of the site. There's also an effective search engine. Once inside the site, in various zones, IslamiCity can be easily navigated via the hyperlinked top bar, and various sidebars.

SPECIAL FEATURES

Devotion (linked on the left-hand side bar) features a substantial library of information central to Muslim faith, including prayer times, recitations of the Qur'an from noted exponents, and a recitation competition featuring children and young adults. Click on the Qur'an link, and a hyperlinked list of verses from the Revelation appears. Choose a section and a page will appear in the original Arabic, with options to view an English translation of the meaning or hear the verse recited (using RealPlayer).

Mosque (linked at the top of the index page) contains a series of links to pages of information about Islam, including material aimed at non-Muslim readers. Understanding Islam and Muslims is a succinct series of 22 slides, taking readers through the very basic principles of Muslim faith. Pillars discusses the Five Pillars of Islam in a short illustrated essay.

Cyber TV (linked at the top of the index page) offers various channels of Islamic content (using RealPlayer), including live and recorded broadcasts from Mecca and Medina, often taken from satellite broadcasts. Audio-visual quality can be variable, but the material is certainly atmospheric and offers insight into Muslim faith and practices. Channel 25 contains a beautiful slide show of Virtual Mosques, accompanied by a high-quality audio call to prayer.

OTHER FEATURES

IslamiCity Baz@r is advertised in the right-hand sidebars, and offers a wide range of Islamic products. These include Qur'ans (in printed and CDRom formats), books, video (including children's titles), and Gifts. IslamiCity provides secure server software for credit card orders, a shopping cart, and clearly explains its sales arrangements under the Policy section. IslamiCity also features an Ask the Imam service, where questions can be submitted to an expert, or previous answers viewed through access to the database.

IslamiCity is a well-managed website, offering detailed perspectives on Muslim faith, from introductory level to advanced.

www.al-islam.org/
Al-Islam

Overall rating: ★ ★ ★ ★			
Classification:	Information	**Readability:**	★ ★ ★ ★
Updating:	Regularly	**Reliability:**	★ ★ ★ ★
Navigation:	★ ★ ★ ★	**Speed:**	★ ★ ★

(INT)

Clear and easy to navigate, this well-designed and thoughtful site introduces aspects of Shia Islam, incorporating its perspective on religious leadership, interpretation of the Qur'an, and relations with other branches of Islamic belief. Al-Islam is organised by the Ahlul Bayt Digital Islamic Library Project, established in 1998, which have built up a substantial and technologically competent set of pages. Navigation is easy, and the site downloads quickly. Adobe Acrobat readers are required for some of the more detailed content. Icons on the front page indicate the nine key categories, which are highlighted and linked throughout the site on the top bar. The site is searchable from the front page.

SPECIAL FEATURES

Beginner's Introduction discusses the origins of Islam from a Shia perspective. Common Misconceptions includes a short article on Islam and the Question of Violence, while Islamic FAQs explores key issues of faith and identity.

Islamic Gallery is located in the Art section of Beliefs and Practices, and is particularly rich. Its Audio Library contains very long lectures, probably not of interest to the general surfer. However, the excellent Photos and Artwork section contains a host of Islamic calligraphy and architecture. There is a gallery of information on specific Shia sacred sites such as Karbala and Kufa, as well as sites 'shared' with Sunni Muslims. These important places of pilgrimage are illustrated with thumbnail GIFs, which can be enlarged. Virtual Worlds could not be opened. The Video Clips are primarily lectures, although there are two extracts from the film of the life of Prophet Muhammad, which require RealPlayer to view. Kids Korner contains books from a Shia perspective, including the lives of prophets and imams (religious leaders). There's a wide selection of pictures (involving substantial download time) presented as thumbnails, including more than 50 of praying, a remarkable 650-plus of good and bad behaviour, and more than 70 assorted depictions of Satan and other 'monsters'.

OTHER FEATURES

Beliefs and Practices goes slightly deeper into comparative religion, the relationship between Shia and Sunni Muslims, philosophy, and spirituality.

Quick Links (at the top of the front page) offers a drop-down menu which delves deeper into Al-Islam's content, linking to an encyclopedia and interpretations of Islamic laws.

In a Nutshell (highlighted on the drop-down menu) is useful if you don't want to do all of your reading about Shia Islam on screen. It incorporates a series of factsheets on different aspects of belief, and can be downloaded using Acrobat or Microsoft Word (for Internet Explorer 5 users).

While some of Al-Islam's content is aimed directly at Shia Muslims, there is also much to gain on the site for general surfers from other religious and/or cultural backgrounds.

www.islamonline.net/English/
Islam Online

Overall rating: ★★★★			
Classification:	Information	Readability:	★★★★
Updating:	Regularly	Reliability:	★★★★★
Navigation:	★★★★★	Speed:	★★★★

QAT

This is an important recent introduction to Islam's representation in cyberspace. The front page contains links to all the key areas of the site: News, Politics, Economics, Society, Entertainment, and Health and Science, together with a substantial section on specific aspects of Islam. These are accessed by the side bar, or by scrolling down the front page. The site is searchable via the window on the top left of the front page. There is also an Arabic version of the site.

SPECIAL FEATURES

Discover Islam is an introductory guide to the faith, broken down into key areas. Start on Exploring Islam, and work through by pressing the 'next' button at the end of the page.

Hajj is a comprehensive resource on the pilgrimage, explaining its ritualistic and historical/religious significance. There are plans to add media clips to these pages.

Qur'an is a searchable database of the Revelation. It is comprehensive, offering RealPlayer extracts and an introductory commentary on each surah (chapter), together with comparative translations from different English sources. However, the audio player will only play one verse from a surah at a time. There is no subject listing, although every surah is listed, and the database can provide a keyword search.

Fatwa Bank is an ongoing, regularly updated collection of 'fatwas' or religious opinions on a wide range of subjects, provided by 'experts' in Islamic jurisprudence. Questions can be emailed in, or dialogue initiated when the discussion is 'live'. Click on Ask the Scholar on the left-hand side bar, then click Recent Sessions to see a list of guest scholars. Click on 'fatwa' beside a name to view the dialogue. Alternatively, the Fatwa Bank is searchable if there is a particular subject you are interested in. The topics that have been discussed include many questions on relationships, together with aspects of interpretation.

Islam Online is notable for its high degree of interactivity via 'live dialogue' with scholars and experts on Islam.

www.arches.uga.edu/~godlas/
Islamic Studies, Islam, Arabic, and Religion

Overall rating: ★ ★ ★ ★

Classification:	Portal	Readability:	★ ★ ★
Updating:	Regularly	Reliability:	★ ★ ★
Navigation:	★ ★ ★	Speed:	★ ★ ★ ★

US

American academic Alan Godlas has produced this useful portal to different areas of Muslim faith, which is regularly updated. The front page contains links to 12 main areas of the site, which in turn present a choice selection of annotated URLs. Also highlighted are new additions, demonstrating the range of websites associated with Islam. We were particularly taken with the external link to the Islamic rock band Dr. Jihad and the Intellectual Muslim Guerillas, whose melodic and lyrically provocative work can be downloaded using MP3.

SPECIAL FEATURES

Muslim World Music is located on the Islamic Art, Music and Architecture around the Word page. 'Music' is perhaps an ambiguous term here, as it incorporates the atmospheric chanting especially associated with Sufism, together with recitals of the Qur'an, and examples of music from Pakistan, Iran, Turkey, Kurdistan, and Malaysia. This is a fascinating introduction into contemporary Muslim religious expression. Unfortunately, the Egypt link was broken, but the Qawwali link is recommended, taking the surfer to the spiritually refreshing music of Nusrat Fateh Ali Khan.

Sufism is a hyperlinked essay on aspects of Islamic mysticism, transporting the reader on an historical and global journey, while explaining terminology and the theoretical frameworks of belief.

Perhaps a little heavy going for some casual surfers, but those seeking further online information about the details of Islamic practice would do well to visit this site, which provides useful links to a wealth of knowledge available on the internet.

www.ummah.net
Islamic Gateway

Overall rating: ★ ★ ★			
Classification:	Information	Readability:	★ ★ ★
Updating:	Regularly	Reliability:	★ ★ ★
Navigation:	★ ★ ★	Speed:	★ ★ ★

UK

Although international in orientation, Islamic Gateway contains areas of particular relevance to sectors within Britain's Muslim communities, and can be helpful in providing alternative perspectives to particular issues. The side bar is linked to the main areas of Islamic Gateway, which acts as a 'host' to different Muslim interests. Sometimes the views can be controversial, and elements hidden within the overall site have a militant feel to them (for example in the Action zone). These can be found through the site map, but should not distract from the content that can be found elsewhere. The front page undergoes regular adjustment, depending on the time of year.

SPECIAL FEATURES

Ramadan is a first-rate resource on the month of fasting. It provides explanations of the religious background to this central tenet of Islam. There are original programs to download, in order to calculate the moon sighting times required during Ramadan, and assorted other programs relating to prayer calculations for the entire year. Moon sighting has become a controversial issue in the UK, primarily associated with the veracity of moon sighting reports (understandable given the British weather!). This page attempts to defuse the situation, giving astronomical data, and a vast archive of other background information to Ramadan.

OTHER FEATURES

Family Page is an interesting cultural-religious collection of links, notably to 12 cookbooks! If you have ever wondered about the background to Muslim names, they can be looked up through this page.

IGCD offers you the chance to buy a CDRom of the site, which can be browsed offline (saving expensive phone bills!)

An ambitious resource aimed at Muslims in the UK, with much to offer other surfers.

OTHER SITES ABOUT ISLAM

Islamic Sufi Orders on the World Wide Web
http://homepages.haqq.com.au/salam/sufilinks/
This is a helpful jump page to a selection of mysticism-related links, and explanations relating to various orders, produced in a user-friendly format. Several have brief introductions, outlining historical and religious origins, and the selection includes groups in African, Asian, and European contexts.

Naqshbandi Sufi Way
www.naqshbandi.org/
There are many sites devoted to Sufism (or Islamic mysticism) on the internet. This site provides an introduction to an important mystical order, with photographs and an audio file of the pledge of allegiance to its 'shaykh'. The order can be studied in more detail through its library of teachings. Titles include 'Escaping from Shaytan' (Satan), 'Swallow Your Anger. Then digest it' and 'Knowledge from Divine Presence'.

Peter Saunders
www.ummah.net/sanders/
British photographer Peter Saunders, whose career includes taking pictures of the Rolling Stones, has travelled the world focusing his lenses on Muslims and Islamic societies. One result has been this excellent archive of commercial, copyrighted photography. As a Muslim, Saunders has been granted unique access to sites and people, including the Ka'ba in Mecca. The only drawback of this site is its application of frames, which makes browsing awkward.

The Sun's House
http://irna.com/occasion/ertehal/index-e.htm
This is an archive of material on Ayatollah Khomeini, with sayings, a biography, and useful English-language video clips from a variety of sources. This include clips of Khomeini's arrival in Tehran during the 'Islamic Revolution', and documentary archival material relating to his role as religious leader in Iran. This site is linked to Iran's Islamic Republic News Agency.

Virtually Islamic
www.virtuallyislamic.com
The author's own commentary on Islam in cyberspace, containing articles, news and substantial links.

judaism

http://aish.com/
Aish HaTorah

Overall rating: ★ ★ ★ ★ ★			
Classification:	Information	**Readability:**	★ ★ ★ ★
Updating:	Regularly	**Reliability:**	★ ★ ★ ★ ★
Navigation:	★ ★ ★ ★	**Speed:**	★ ★ ★ ★ ★
UK			

Aish HaTorah ('man of the law') is one of the most effective religious sites on the web, with much to interest those seeking knowledge on phenomena associated with (aspects of) Judaism. The site has a magazine format, with regularly changed articles on Judaism-related themes. The site can be searched from the bar at the top of the page. On entry to the site, scroll down the page via links to areas such as Issues, Family, Dating and Spirituality. Below these sections, there are 14 other major sections, ranging from Jewish Literacy to Holocaust Studies. There are links to Hebrew, Spanish and Russian versions of the site, and a selection of free newsletters can be obtained by email.

SPECIAL FEATURES

Window on the Wall, which is linked on the front page, feeds from a live 24-hour webcam on the Western Wall in Jerusalem (refresh your page occasionally to observe the changing view). This section links into key conceptual areas relating to the Aish HaTorah's particular interpretation of Judaism, which focuses on preventing assimilation and promoting Jewish identity; specific prayers are provided, for example for good health, for the sick, for livelihood and for a safe journey. There is a discussion on conversion to Judaism, and a message can be emailed for insertion in the wall. The wall can be viewed, accompanied by appropriate music (from the menu box below the image of the wall).

The Tunnel Tour While obviously presenting its own opinion relating to the controversial opening of the labyrinth under Jerusalem, this is an excellent teaching tool, making good use of web-media. It includes a timeline, chronicling the history of the Western Wall from the time of the Patriarchs through to the present day, and speculating on the historical significance of the tunnels. This works via a series of frames, through which the route of the tunnel can be traced. The surfer can also view a 360-degree panoramic view of the wall. Click on the sidebar on the Easy Guide to the Tunnel Tour to ensure that you have the correct software installed. You'll need RealPlayer to hear a commentary, and if your browser does not support Java applets required for the 360-degree views, then there is a link to download an appropriate PhotoVista plug-in.

Ask the Rabbi is an opportunity to ask questions to the resident Aish Rabbi, through filling in a form. This can be done anonymously. There is also a fascinating archive of more than 360 previous questions, from afterlife to Yom Kippur, which must have stretched the Rabbi's knowledge! This archive can be searched for a particular theme, or for the curious passer-by the entire listing can be browsed.

OTHER FEATURES

The site has a regularly updated Jewish Issues section, and the Spirituality section provides articles on contemporary approaches to belief. The section on Kabbalah (*sic*) (Jewish Mysticism), accessed via the Spirituality button, was very accessible and potentially controversial: 'Kabbala is the Torah's expression of the way the world works. Removed from its source, it's a whole lot of rubbish.' There are some commercial links, and a hyperlink to SpeedDating, an online series of events for Jewish singles.

This is an excellent portal, primarily linked to Aish HaTorah material. The bold and imaginative content make it an essential visit, although its perspective may not appeal to all Jewish surfers.

www.jewishfamily.com/

JewishFamily

Overall rating: ★ ★ ★			
Classification:	Information	**Readability:**	★ ★ ★ ★
Updating:	Regularly	**Reliability:**	★ ★ ★ ★
Navigation:	★ ★ ★ ★ ★	**Speed:**	★ ★ ★ ★ ★

US

This is a well-designed and absorbing magazine format site, part of the Jewz.com group (also see their site www.interfaithfamily.com), with a wealth of helpful and interesting information. The entry page makes navigation very easy. At the top of the page are symbols: place your pointer on them, and a text label appears on the right of the screen indicating their meaning. Categories include Jewish Celebrations, Families, Lifestyles, Culture and Your Voices. There's also a search box, if you are seeking something specific. Alternatively, scroll down the page and select from the list of articles or video material (requires RealPlayer). The site states: 'JewishFamily strives to help families apply Judaism and Jewish values to their everyday lives and to be a source of user-friendly, family-oriented information and entertainment. We hope to provide a Jewish link to families who may not feel comfortable in traditional Jewish organizations.'

SPECIAL FEATURE

Dear Rabbi The rabbi in question is Rabbi Bradley Shavit Artson, and he gets to tackle a broad range of problems. This is part of the JewishFamily site, and this section includes responses to some interesting questions on contemporary issues. Conversion to Judaism (from Christianity and Islam) is discussed, together with identity concerns based on raising children within different faith structures (Two Faiths and a Confused Child); Conservative

Conversion and Orthodox Relatives provides examples of the pressures placed on converts.

OTHER FEATURES

Jewish Celebrations is a lively and topical selection of articles. On a visit during Hanukkah, topics included issues relating to how to deal with Hanukkah and Christmas in interfaith families; that is, where one partner is Jewish, and the other Christian. There was a section entitled 'Is Santa Jewish?'. There is a substantial amount of homely advice in this section, which makes for a fascinating read.

Lifestyles is divided into Health, Food and Travel sections. They're all regularly updated, often in relation to the Jewish calendar: for example, the Food section had recipes for Hanukkah, including some tempting latkes.

Whatever your religious backgrounds or interests, Jewish Family offers a wealth of unique, and occasionally idiosyncratic, cultural and 'religious' material which makes a welcome change from some of the uniformity presented by portals.

www.chabad.org/
Chabad-Lubavitch in Cyberspace

Overall rating: ★ ★ ★			
Classification:	Information	**Readability:**	★ ★ ★
Updating:	Regularly	**Reliability:**	★ ★ ★
Navigation:	★ ★ ★	**Speed:**	★ ★ ★ ★

UK

Chabad-Lubavitch in Cyberspace started promoting their interpretation of Judaism on the Internet in 1988: 'The major thrust of Chabad-Lubavitch focuses on observing for oneself and transmitting to others the beauty, depth, awareness and joy inherent in the Torah-true way of life.' Content can be found in nine languages, including Hebrew and English. The front page loads quickly, and you don't have to be a follower to appreciate this site, which offers information from basic level upwards. Menus for the site can be found at the top of the page (left click the down arrow on 'Choose One' to reveal a variety of categories). Alternatively, scroll down the page.

SPECIAL FEATURES

Front page features a link to a Chassidic (*sic*) thought of the day in English (updated daily). Alternatively, you can listen to other readings and prayers on audio files, which require RealPlayer.

OTHER FEATURES

Sections include Daily Lessons, Weekly Texts, FAQ, and information about religious leaders (Rebbe), including Baal Shem Tov and Menachem Mendel Schneerson. The site includes a tribute to the 'Virtual Rabbi of Cyberspace', Yosef Y Kazen (1954-1999), who established the website as a conduit of Chabad-Lubavitch perspectives. Hasidic women's pages include opinions on 'Chasidic Feminists' and

'Chasidic Women Earning PhDs'. Surfers, whether Jewish or not, can send a request to the late Rebbe for intercession (include parents' names on your email). Elsewhere, there is even a Rabbi Riddle section.

As one of the original religious sites on the internet, Chabad-Lubavitch in Cyberspace's extensive experience of the medium is fully demonstrated on this site, which is easy to navigate and full of interesting content, although there were some broken links at the time of writing.

www.jewfaq.org/
Judaism 101

Overall rating: ★ ★ ★			
Classification:	Encyclopedia	**Readability:**	★ ★ ★ ★
Updating:	Regularly	**Reliability:**	★ ★ ★ ★
Navigation:	★ ★ ★	**Speed:**	★ ★ ★ ★ ★

US

Judaism 101 is an online encyclopedia, compiled by Tracey Rich, that is easy to navigate and worthy of several visits. It covers many aspects of Jewish belief in detail, and the material is graded into categories of Beginner, Intermediate and Advanced. The emphasis is on so-called Orthodox Judaism, although derivations are also discussed. Judaism 101's advantage is a clear and concise introduction to Judaism, through which it is easy to progress to an 'Advanced' stage of knowledge. The opening page offers advice on Judaism 101, including how the material is categorised and should be approached. A frames version of the site can be accessed.

SPECIAL FEATURE

Table of Contents introduces the substantial amount of information to get through on Judaism 101! This is categorised under ten headings, which feature on the sidebar buttons, and on the page's scrollable text. The material covers a variety of interesting topics, including What is Halakhah (Jewish Law)?, Kosher Sex, and Life Cycle. These and other issues are represented in hypertext essays, occasionally illustrated by animated GIFs and sound files, which integrate well with each other. There are no great surprises on the site, but the content is accessible. Pages are often quite short, and presented in straightforward English. The entire site can be downloaded as a zip file, and is also searchable via a link on the contents page.

A useful entry point to learning about Judaism, or discovering information about a particular aspect of belief, although content can be dry at times and greater direction to detailed sources would be useful.

www.zipple.com
Zipple

Overall rating: ★ ★ ★			
Classification:	Information	**Readability:**	★ ★ ★
Updating:	Regularly	**Reliability:**	★ ★ ★
Navigation:	★ ★ ★ ★	**Speed:**	★ ★ ★ ★

US

Among the numerous other gateways for Judaism in cyberspace, Zipple represents itself as the 'Online Jewish Resource to explore Judaism, Israel, and the Holocaust'. Zipple is a massive venture, with religious, cultural and community components. Zipple can be quite daunting to surf, and is at times complex to navigate; information overload is a distinct possibility. However, it is also fun to visit. Founded in 1998 by Jory Rozner, Zipple had an extensive makeover at the end of 2000, substantially improving navigation and usability. The name Zipple doesn't have any intrinsic meaning, although Rozner thought it sounded Yiddish. 'She decided she wanted Zipple to stand for fun, hip, cool, and Jewish. Zipple.com it was.' Rozner designed Zipple to have a broad appeal: 'She didn't limit herself to specific affiliations (Orthodox, Conservative, Reform) or specific ideologies or specific anything. She didn't even limit herself to thinking only about the Jewish community – because she realized that plenty of non-Jews have an interest in things Jewish'.

Zipple has adopted purple as its key colour, and you enter into a magazine format, which is dominated by daily updated news pages (sourced primarily from the Jewish Telegraph). The site is searchable, from a box at the top of the main page. The side bar links to key areas, primarily of interest to US surfers (Business, Get a Job! and the Events Calendar). We found that the best place to navigate from was the Site Map, linked on the beige banner near the top of the page.

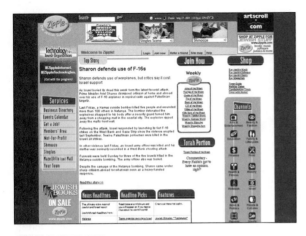

SPECIAL FEATURES

Religion Accessed through the site map or search engine, this is an excellent hyperlinked resource of news and archive materials. The page is easy to read, and contains content of interest to specialists and the curious alike. It illustrates the rich choice of materials on Judaism available, including four Ask the Rabbis, five Jewish Law sites, and 20 specialist Kabbalah sites!

Shmooze is indicated on the main page's top banner as one of three key areas of Zipple interest: the Singles Scene, an online store, and the Shmooz chat room. Registration via an online form is required to participate in these areas of the site. The process takes about five minutes: the form states that a dialling code and state is required for US/Canadian surfers. Leaving those boxes blank means that the form comes back to you with unfilled fields, which is frustrating if you live outside of North America: to get around this, try putting a 508 code in the dialling area, and choose a state for the relevant box. Take care to check the box regarding registering for the mailing list, to avoid receiving unnecessary spam mail (it's a good idea to use a junk mail

web address for such forms). Confirmation email was sent, allowing entry into the members' area. This includes an email service, and an invitation to the Scene Singles area. Shmooze, on the left-hand side bar, offers a choice of formats and speeds for the chat rooms. Discussion Groups lists a variety of areas: Ask the Rabbi was somewhat sparse, but the Jewish Culture and History section had some interesting postings.

OTHER FEATURES

The site map is clear and effective, making this one of the best portals for information on Judaism, a proportion of which is produced by Zipple. Categories include the Holocaust, Learn Yiddish and Hebrew, Holidays (all are listed), and Food. The Weekly Zipple (linked on the left-hand sidebar) includes a Jokes section, with 100 different entries, including Jewish computer jokes and – naturally – Jewish mother jokes. Elsewhere, the Torah portion is updated regularly, and contains a variety of perspectives. The portion we sampled also incorporated jokes and quotations. Zipple hosts special events, encouraging participation at organised times (set your watch to New York). The online store links into designated Amazon.com and other online store pages.

Even if you were not interested in the Jewish singles' scene, Zipple's specialist areas would make an excellent starting point for anyone wanting to learn more about Judaism and Jewish culture.

OTHER SITES ABOUT JUDAISM

A Gateway to the Wisdom of Kabbalah and Chassidut
www.inner.org/
The Gateway includes teachings from Rabbi Yitzhak Ginsburg, providing an overview of Jewish mystical thought (including the Hebrew letters), a glossary of terminology, and samples of Chassidic melodies. The article listing contains responses to contemporary issues. The site links into opportunities to purchase related books and materials.

A Teacher's Guide to the Holocaust
http://fcit.coedu.usf.edu/holocaust/
Produced by the Florida Center for Instructional Technology, this sites provides excellent resources for Holocaust studies, including photographs, video, and music. The timeline is effective, outlining key events, and providing a view of history that goes right through to the present day. The victims' section studies all the groups deemed 'undesirable' by the Nazi regime.

Ethiopian Jewry Page
www.circus.org/nacoej.htm
The situation of Ethiopian Jews (or Falashah) is detailed here, a site with a particular focus on the security of the remaining Jewish population in Ethiopia. The documentation demonstrating their 'official' status as Jews in Israel, as endorsed by the Chief Rabbinate of Israel, is particularly interesting.

Jewish
www.jewish.co.uk
This shares some content with Aish HaTorah (see p.69), and also draws on material from other sites. There is news and views from the Jewish community in Britain, and some original sections. Judaism Today includes a Jewish festivals guide, Shabbos Times and Weekly Torah, and a UK synagogue directory.

Karaite Korner
www.karaite-korner.org/
'Karaites preserve the original religion of the Hebrew Bible, rejecting later innovations such as the Rabbinic Oral Law. Every individual is required to take responsibility for interpreting the Tanach.' This outlines Karaite beliefs effectively, with articles on Karaism v Rabbinism, the 'assumptions' behind Tzitzit (fringes), Tefillin (Phylacteries), and the Karaite perspective on festivals such as Passover Haggadah and Rosh Hashanah (Yom Teruah according to the Karaite). The site also contains detailed information on the sighting of the New Moon (important for prayer and festival days).

Orthodox Union
www.ou.org/
A gateway for orthodox Jews to resources and news, linking into hundreds of related sites (from food to dating). They provide their own Ask the Rabbi service, organised through the Rabbinical Council of in conjunction with the Orthodox Union, the Beth Din of America and Kollel Eretz Hemdah in Jerusalem.

Reform Judaism
http://rj.org/
The Union of American Hebrew Congregations have produced this site, the highlight of which is an Ask the Rabbi section containing over 2,000 archived FAQs and an email form to submit other questions that a surfer might have. Subjects include parenting issues, Jewish life cycle, GodTalk, reform Judaism, choosing Judaism, and choosing the Covenant.

Temple Mount and Land of Israel Faithful Movement
www.templemountfaithful.org/
This site is run by Gershon Salomon, a lecturer in Middle Eastern studies, who also contributes a substantial amount of material on the site. He was an Israeli Army officer, who took part in the 'liberation' of the disputed area of Temple

Mount (illustrated by a photo on the site). The illustrative material includes illustrations of the Second Temple, while the underlying theme of the site is the desire to build a new Temple on the current site of Al Aqsa mosque (the third holiest site in Islam). The Movements objectives are clearly stated: 'Liberating the Temple Mount from Arab (Islamic) occupation. The Dome of the Rock and the Al Aqsa mosque were placed on this Jewish or Biblical holy site as a specific sign of Islamic conquest and domination. The Temple Mount can never be consecrated to the Name of God without removing these pagan shrines. It has been suggested that they be removed, transferred to and rebuilt at Mecca.'

The Jewish Dance
http://members.xoom.com/lamadorje/dancing.html
This site overloads your hard drive with dancing Rabbis and other rotating Judaic images, but it's a fun way of exploring Judaism and the hundreds of potential sites available. Accompany your surfing with a variety of traditional tunes!

The Nizkor Project
www.nizkor.org/
It's difficult to make a choice of Holocaust-related sites, given the plethora of worthy and important materials available online. The Nizkor Project is geared around education, and challenges both misrepresentation of the Holocaust, and Holocaust denial. It includes material on the death camps, articles on 'revisionism' and 'denial', and links to the Shofar FTP archives.

Torat-Chayim
www.jtsa.edu/lists/tor-ch/
Conservative Judaism presented by Toray-Chayim (Living Torah), linking into several discussion groups. There's a listing of Hebrew terminology, instructions on How to Lay Tefillin, and a curious page on cyber-sin(!).

Virtual Center of the Sephardic Community
www.bsz.org/
The Virtual Center is particularly impressive for its historical pages, which contain histories relating to Sephardic Jewry in locations as diverse as Brooklyn and Syria, together with personal histories and photographs. The musical pages include a variety of recordings, using traditional instrumentation. The site links into a variety of Sephardic synagogues in the USA and elsewhere.

Yashanet
www.yashanet.com/
Yashanet is a library containing Torah study material, Historical Studies 'about how the teachings of Scripture, Yeshua and His Torah-observant followers "evolved" into today's Christianity', and Messianic Studies. The site includes an attempt to classify Jews according to Torah observance.

other beliefs

Other Beliefs reflects some of the diversity in the religions of the world, consisting of worldviews that are drawn from diverse cultures, philosophies, and spiritual perspectives. This section has been divided into four parts, which are in fact inter-related, and demonstrate the dangers of placing beliefs into rigid categories: the Prophets, Saints and Thinkers and Gurus and New Religious Movements sections are particularly closely related, although the latter section represents more modern religious innovations, and for adherents there may be some blurring between a prophet and a guru. Both may be seen as intermediaries with the transcendent, possessing qualities that some may label as divine or superhuman.

Defining a New Religious Movement (NRM) can cause problems, but so do other terms such as alternative religion, cult or sect. An NRM indicates origins outside of conventional religious contexts, and is the preferred term here. The terms 'sect' and 'cult' have negative implications and may be applied stereotypically to non-conventional beliefs, suggesting fanaticism, brainwashing, and other nefarious deeds. The roles of charismatic leaders within these beliefs have been questioned by so-called cult watching, counter cult and/or anti-cult groups (which may be accessed via the General Portals section). To some interpreters, NRMs may also exist within one of the world religions discussed in the earlier chapter (for example, the Unification Church has been described as an NRM and cult, and may have fitted in this section). Remember that, depending on the definition of cult, the world's 'major' religions may have also held that status early in their history.

While it may be important to be aware of such issues, this should not detract from this rich and varied area of religious cyberspace. Many other beliefs are making good use of the internet, especially as a networking tool and means of attracting new followers. Many regularly update their pages, drawing on magazine-style formats, and investing substantial sums to produce easy-to-use websites that can be a joy to navigate. The integration of notions of religious experience into hypertext is especially prevalent within the imaginative contexts of certain other beliefs, and there are numerous opportunities to interact with followers or obtain more detailed information. Not all the sites reviewed are necessarily 'official', and this suggests that there can be several different approaches to specific other beliefs.

The other two sections in this chapter contain particularly interesting approaches to the use of the internet by other religions: Mythology, Pantheism, Polytheism and the Spirit World has some dynamic examples of how the net can be applied as an educational and community resource, and provides pages which represent innovative libraries of materials that are unpublished or difficult to access elsewhere. Religions that are now effectively been lost to the world still maintain a place in cyberspace. The Esoteric and New Age section indicates that interactivity and spirituality can combine with surprising results (to the uninitiated), and that the diversity of New Age worldviews which are significant to individuals is well-represented online, even if they cannot always be found within the textbook! There are hundreds of possible sites for inclusion within this section, demonstrating that the quest for religious experience has gone beyond convention for many esoterically and spiritually minded individuals. Aspects of these beliefs have been drawn upon by other religions (and vice versa), and form part of everyday life for many people, even if they are not always described as being 'religious' in orientation.

prophets, saints and thinkers

bahá'í

The Bahá'í are well served by the internet, with thousands of pages covering a variety of topics, from focused academic studies through to resources for casual and non-Bahá'í surfers, with plenty of networking between the sites.

www.bahai.com/ or www.bahai.org			
Bahai World			
Overall rating: ★ ★ ★			
Classification: Portal		**Readability:**	★ ★
Updating: Regularly		**Reliability:**	★ ★
Navigation: ★ ★ ★ ★ ★		**Speed:**	★ ★
(INT)			

Bahá'í World is a hub to significant resources, all of which can be accessed from the front page. While a proportion of the content is aimed at existing Bahá'ís, there is much of interest to the general surfer.

SPECIAL FEATURES

Bahá'í Writings is a detailed archive of information on the Bahá'í, including the sacred writings of the religion's founder, Bahá'u'lláh. Titles include the Kitáb-i-Aqdas (The Most Holy Book), Epistle to the Son of the Wolf, and The Hidden Words of Bahá'u'lláh.

OTHER FEATURES

Spiritual Truths contains ten key headings, including The Oneness of Religion, God, Faith and Immortality, and the Changeless Faith of God. These are primarily in the form of essays, containing occasional hyperlinks.

Bahá'í World is an official introduction to Bahá'í religious beliefs, presenting the history of the religion, and key elements of sacred concepts. The associated Bahá'í World Magazine contains articles introducing Bahá'í concepts (in Bulgarian, Chinese, Italian, Spanish, French and English).

Somewhat dry in content, and slow to download, the site appears to be preaching to the converted.

OTHER BAHAI SITES

The Bahá'í Community of the United Kingdom
www.bahai.org.uk/
For optimum navigability, the site utilises Flash to enter, although if you don't have the software there is a non-Flash enabled link at the bottom on the front page. Place the cursor over one of the seven stars on the front page, which lead to the main sections of the site; these include General Information, Links to the Bahá'í Community, Administrative Information, and Selections from Bahá'í Holy Writings. However, the contents were rather sparse at the time of writing, making this a site in progress at present.

Bahá'í Faith Index
www.bcca.org/~cvoogt/
This could be the answer to any question you may have about Bahá'í religion. It's an encyclopedic resource, in 35 languages, from Arabic to Welsh, Maori to Esperanto, Faeroese to Icelandic. There are more than 3,000 links to varied Bahá'í pages, for those seeking to develop their knowledge in the subject. Downloads require Adobe Acrobat.

Confucianism

This is a difficult subject to locate user-friendly online materials. Many sites require specialist knowledge, a grasp of Chinese, and appropriate browsers.

| **www.easternreligions.com/cframe.html** | | | |
Confucius Page			
Overall rating: ★ ★			
Classification:	Information	**Readability:**	★ ★
Updating:	Occasionally	**Reliability:**	★ ★
Navigation:	★ ★ ★	**Speed:**	★ ★ ★
US			

This is the most accessible introduction to Confucius (551-479 BC) on the internet. The main page has a picture of 'the historical Ch'iu K'ung, who became known as K'ung-fu'-tse, or K'ung the Philosopher, whom we call Confucius'. Below the introduction are the key areas of Confucius' life and links

to other sites (includes a broken link). The left-hand side bar takes you to other areas of the Look Within website. A major revision of the entire site is planned for 2001.

SPECIAL FEATURES

Text on Confucius outlines his life, morals, wisdom, analects and other biographical features. It's very much an overview, lacking detailed references, but useful for beginners.

A basic introduction, which will set the reader up for further detailed reading on Confucius.

OTHER SITES OF CONFUSIANISM

Confucianism
www.askasia.org/frclasrm/readings/r000004.htm
This is an article written by Judith A. Berling for the Asia Society's Focus on Asian Studies, which discussed the origins of Confucianism and Confucius's ethical vision.

Confucius Publishing House
www.confucius.org/english/lange.htm
Selected quotations from the Master, available in 16 languages, together with a Picture Archive of associated objects.

jain

www.jainworld.com/			
Jainworld			
Overall rating: ★★			
Classification: Information	**Readability:**	★★	
Updating: Occasionally	**Reliability:**	★★★	
Navigation: ★★★	**Speed:**	★	
UAE US			

The site is easy to navigate, with key areas below the main picture. The right-hand links offer opportunities to hear recitals giving obeisance to the Adorable, the Emancipated, the Preceptors, the Saints and the Deans (these are small files, using Windows Media Player).

SPECIAL FEATURES

Philosophy introduces important areas of Jainism, including the emphasis on self-restraint and non-violence. Devotional Songs offers RealPlayer recordings of prayer, with explanations, translation and illustrations.

Education is directed at Jain youth, but may be helpful for those seeking a user-friendly introduction to Jainism. The Alphabet was colourful and informative.

Literature presents a variety of materials, such as First Steps to Jainism, as online books which allow deeper exploration of the faith.

Jainworld is worthy of exploration, but navigation can be difficult, and download times frustrating.

sikhism

www.sikhs.org			
Sikhism Home Page			
Overall rating: ★★★★			
Classification: Information	**Readability:**	★★★★	
Updating: Occasionally	**Reliability:**	★★★★	
Navigation: ★★★	**Speed:**	★★★	
CAN			

Founded in 1994, this was one of the earliest Sikh websites, and is still a very useful resource for exploring Sikhism from diverse religious, cultural and historical angles. Readers are greeted with a short prayer on accessing this site. Click on the main graphic to reach the front page; key zones are represented with appropriate symbols.

SPECIAL FEATURES

Sikh Way of Life contains a number of insightful sections: Gurdwara describes Sikh temples, and a Virtual Tour of the Golden Temple complex in Amritsar, where panoramic views can be obtained, allows the browser to 'experience' the holiest shrine in Sikhism. Particularly interesting in the Ceremonies and Festivals section is the account of a Sikh Wedding; each stage is presented with an explanation and photographs (unfortunately, it is impossible to download the atmosphere or culinary delights).

Sikh Gurus, Saints, and Gurdwaras can be accessed through clicking on the kirpan (dagger). The hypertext listing of ten Gurus presents each master's biography, anecdotal material, and an artistic impression; nine saints' lives are also presented.

OTHER FEATURES

Philosophy and Scriptures includes an impressive resource base, notably the Sri Guru Granth Sahib. This central Sikhism text is available in English translations, with searchable indices. The merits of various editions are discussed. Resources include Audio Prayers, such as the Ardas common prayer, daily prayers, and the marriage ceremony. Nitnem Banis, daily Sikh prayers, can be heard in Punjabi. There is also a glossary of Sikh terminology.

This well-organised site, containing interesting images and graphics, is an excellent introduction to Sikhism.

OTHER SIKH SITES

Sikh Network

www.sikhnet.com/

Online resources include Gurmukhi, Punjabi and Hindi fonts for use when studying the Guru Granth Sahib – which itself can be downloaded in its entirety in various versions. You can also download a questionnaire, designed to determine 'how close you are to the principles of Sikh religion founded by Sri Guru Nanak Dev Ji'. Based in the United States, Sikhnet also offers Sikh email, a radio channel (down at the time of visiting), and a discussion forum which is designed to be a contribution 'to the sacred space we hold for Sikhnet on the Web'.

Sikh Seek

www.sikhseek.com/

If you haven't found what you were looking for through the above sites, then take a look at Sikh Seek, the 'Sikhism Guide for finding anything Sikh'. Among the 450-plus selections are links to Sikh matrimonial services, Punjabi culture, and Yoga.

shintoism

http://shinto.org/menu-e.html			
International Shinto Foundation			
Overall rating: ★ ★			
Classification:	Information	Readability:	★ ★
Updating:	Regularly	Reliability:	★ ★
Navigation:	★ ★ ★	Speed:	★ ★
(JAP)			

Based primarily in Japan, Shinto followers may also be Buddhist or Christian. This site (also available in Japanese) provides a concise introduction to the faith.

SPECIAL FEATURES

What is Shinto? briefly discusses the historical origins of the religion, its links with Buddhism, and its association with Japanese identity.

Shinto and the Sacred Dimension of Nature is a more substantial essay, discussing the transformations that have taken place in Shinto beliefs.

More information would have been useful, but this is a serviceable introduction to Shinto faith.

taoism (daoism)

www.edepot.com/taoism.shtml			
Daoism Depot			
Overall rating: ★ ★			
Classification: Information		**Readability:**	★ ★
Updating: Occasionally		**Reliability:**	★ ★
Navigation: ★ ★ ★		**Speed:**	★ ★ ★
n/a			

This is a Flash enabled page, complete with background music. Scroll down to the rotating Yin Yang menu, which is divided into Contemplate, Communicate and Related Subjects.

SPECIAL FEATURES

Introduction to Daoism offers a concise primer on the historical figures, deities, symbols, and origins of the faith. The text is is clear, and will help you through the rest of the site if you are new to Taoism.

Introduction to Daoist Scriptures includes a discussion on key texts, and a hyperlinked listing at the end of the page taking the surfer to important titles (in Chinese and English).

OTHER FEATURES

The Virtual Daoist Temple has some distinctly un-Daoist comments amidst the religious messages that had been left, suggesting the section requires closer management. Live Chat is available, although there were no other Daoists online when we visited. The site links into the Wandering Daoist webring, which in turn links to to more than 200 sites.

Text only, with limited interactivity, but a useful starting point for wandering Daoists.

OTHER TAO SITES

Tao Te Ching
www.clas.ufl.edu/users/gthursby/taoism/ttcstan2.htm
This translation of the Tao Te Ching by Stan Rosenthal is designed for entry level students, and comes with an explanatory introduction.

I Ching Empower Tool
http://ourworld.compuserve.com/homepages/empowerto ols/iching.htm
This computer program allows for consultation with an online oracle: 'Ask the I Ching oracle your most intimate questions and receive immediate, detailed answers.' Hexagrams can be interpreted, and you can conduct your own consultation, if you have three similar coins. You can also download shareware (for Windows) that throws virtual coins, and offers additional analysis.

The Abode of the Eternal Tao
www.abodetao.com/
Taoism's 'ancient shamanic roots' preceded the writing of the Tao Te Ching by Lao Tzu, whose origins and status are shrouded in mystery. This site attempts to address some of the issues, with its What is Taoism? section of FAQs. This is primarily a commercial site which also publicises books (with sample chapters) and other products (with secure shopping).

zoroastrianism

www.zoroastrian.net/
Zoroastrian Net

Overall rating: ★ ★ ★			
Classification:	Information	Readability:	★ ★ ★
Updating:	Regularly	Reliability:	★ ★ ★
Navigation:	★ ★ ★ ★	Speed:	★ ★ ★

(IND)

Zoroastrianism dates back thousands of years, and has been influential on other religions, and is now embracing the internet in order to network disparate communities across the world. Zoroastrian Net seeks to be 'a single source of information for community news, history, religious information, guidance on ceremonies, and everything else which is relevant to Zoroastrians. It will also build a library of a large number of books, many of them of old and almost forgotten, but a part of the literature no less'. This is still a site in development, but easy to navigate in its present form via the links at the top of the page. Several sections are aimed specifically at the global Zoroastrian community, but there is plenty of interesting content for the general surfer. The site offers free @zoroastrian.net email. There are regularly updated news headlines.

SPECIAL FEATURES

Our Religion contains the Holy Gathas of Prophet Zarathrushtra, explaining the tenets of Zoroastrianism and its ancient origins. Prayers goes into some depth on the theological basis of the faith. The symbolic significance of the calendar is also explained.

OTHER FEATURES

Personal Announcements includes matrimonial notices, from Zoroastrians throughout the world, and information on births and deaths (is longevity a reflection of the Zoroastrian lifestyle?). Send a Zoroastrian Greeting Card offers symbolic emails for every occasion.

A good introduction to Zoroastrianism, also linking to other key pages worldwide.

OTHER ZOROASTRIAN SITES

Avesta
www.avesta.org/avesta.html
Avesta is the most ancient scripture of Zoroastrianism, presented here in its entirety, together with other significant and rare resources for those curious about Zoroastrian religion. Rituals are described, and the front page also indicates friction between different traditional and modernising elements within the belief system.

Traditional Zoroastrianism: Tenets of the Religion
www.ozemail.com.au/~zarathus/tenets33.html
Presenting the ancestral beliefs of Zarathushtri religion, and promoting its continuity in contemporary contexts in India.

gurus & new religious movements

aum shinrikyo

<table>
<tr><td colspan="4">www.aum-shinrikyo.com/english/index.htm
Aum Shinrikyo</td></tr>
<tr><td colspan="4">Overall rating: ★★</td></tr>
<tr><td>Classification:</td><td>Information</td><td>Readability:</td><td>★★</td></tr>
<tr><td>Updating:</td><td>Regularly</td><td>Reliability:</td><td>★★</td></tr>
<tr><td>Navigation:</td><td>★★★</td><td>Speed:</td><td>★★★</td></tr>
<tr><td colspan="4">RUS</td></tr>
</table>

'After cognition of meaning of human experience one is to abandon worldly life in order to surpass a human society, to devote oneself to this totally, to experience one by one worlds higher than Human World, that is Heavens of Degenerated Consciousness, Heavens of Playful Degeneration, Holy Heavens, worlds higher than Holy Heavens, Realm of Non-Form; to estimate, to analyse, to surpass them and to achieve the Great Realm of Total Destruction of Afflictions and Attaining the True Wisdom.'

The apocalyptic religious movement Aum Shinrikyo gained notoriety after their 1994-95 bombing campaign on Tokyo's train network, using sarin poison gas, which left at least a dozen people dead, and hundreds of casualties. The movement was also accused of a campaign of kidnap and murder, and more than 100 followers were arrested. Aum Shinrikyo's leader Asahara Shoko (b.1955) and his followers were indicted, and at the time of writing (2001) were being processed through the Japanese justice system. Aum Shinrikyo manifestos, publicity and tracts are available through the internet, produced both in Japan and elsewhere.

This site describes itself as the official page produced by the Russian branch of the Aum Shinrikyo. Opening it activates an irritating MIDI music file. The site has been substantially improved in its design, however, clearly listing the key areas on the front page with a minimum of graphical accompaniment. It incorporates Messages from the Master, evidence of the Master's 'supernatural powers', the Teaching of Aum Supreme Truth, and Master Shoko Asahara's guide on how to choose your partner by colours. Pick a colour, and the qualities associated with it are revealed. Beware of 'dim dirty violet'...

Aum Shinrikyo followers have produced a clear site through which readers can make up their own minds regarding the role of the cult.

hare krishna

http://chantandbehappy.com/
Krishna Internet Radio Station

Overall rating: ★ ★ ★ ★			
Classification:	Information	**Readability:**	★ ★ ★ ★
Updating:	Regularly	**Reliability:**	★ ★ ★ ★
Navigation:	★ ★ ★ ★	**Speed:**	★ ★ ★ ★ ★

UK

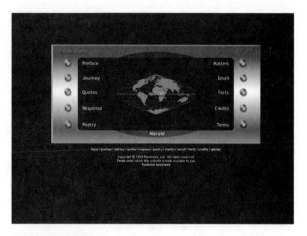

The Krishna Internet Radio Station makes creative use of RealPlayer technology to present its message. The site incorporates devotional music and prayers, mission statements, and lectures by senior Hare Krishna devotees. His Divine Grace AC Bhaktivedanta Swami Prabhupada (1896-1977), founder of Hare Krishna movement, can be heard on the site. The site is easy to navigate, via the side bar, which also contains a drop-down Tune-a-Channel menu. Files can be heard in real time, and/or directly downloaded onto your hard drive. File sizes are given, together with details and explanations of the recordings.

SPECIAL FEATURES

Bhajans (Devotional Songs) uses RealAudio to present the music and hymns regularly used in all International Society for Krishna Consciousness temples. The music crosses styles and formats, from traditional to contemporary.

Learn How to Play the Mrdanga contains detailed lessons on playing the traditional mrdanga drum, starting from scratch. It may be time consuming, but lessons are clear and free, and seem to be a lot of fun. There are plenty of recordings to get you started.

OTHER FEATURES

The Manor contains an archive recorded at Bhaktivedanta Manor, the European Headquarters of the International Society for Krishna Consciousness. The listing includes recordings of lectures, classes, and even a Krishna version of the Canterbury Tales(!). Srila Prabhupada archive includes Everyone of you Become a Guru, Krishna Consciousness is Superior to Mystic Power, Chanting Relieves Pain, and Conversation with George Harrison, John Lennon and Yoko Ono.

The reliance on RealPlayer content may not be to everyone's taste, but the site does provide a rich online Hare Krishna experience.

maharaji

www.maharaji.org/
Maharaji

Overall rating: ★ ★ ★			
Classification: Information	**Readability:**	★ ★	
Updating: Occasionally	**Reliability:**	★ ★	
Navigation: ★ ★ ★	**Speed:**	★ ★ ★ ★	

(IND)

The Maharaji is a spiritual mentor to the Divine Light Mission, which draws its inspiration from elements of Hinduism and Sikhism, and is based around the notion of knowledge passed down by a guru. The pages are nicely designed, although the initial entry to the site is a rare online example of the user agreeing to certain contractual obligations by entering. Don't panic! Legal advice probably isn't necessary, and if you choose to comply you'll discover that the Maharaji is making good use of the medium. You need Flash and QuickTime to hear the music. The present Maharaji designed the website, providing artwork, music, and photos. The site lists previous maharajas (with photos), and quotes from the current Maharaji. Each section is really a sequence of slides on key areas, presenting the Maharaji's personal perspective.

SPECIAL FEATURES

Response has short quotes on Life, Thirst, Time, Hope and Courage, which can be browsed while listening to the Maharaji's music compositions. It would seem from the email responses that many surfers enjoyed their experience at the site.

OTHER FEATURES

Facts provide information on the personal and religious background to the Maharaji.

While the content is sparse in places, there are few other religious websites that are designed by their spiritual mentor in such a 'hands-on' way, giving this site a high curiosity value for the neutral surfer.

OTHER SITES

Elan Vital
www.elanvital.org.uk/
The Maharaji's UK followers have produced an effective website, detailing their activities, and linked to other branches worldwide. It's easy to locate further information about the group, with introductory documents available via Adobe Acrobat Reader or direct email contact.

meher baba

www.avatarmeherbaba.org/
Meher Baba, Avatar of the Age

Overall rating: ★ ★ ★			
Classification:	Information	Readability:	★ ★
Updating:	Occasionally	Reliability:	★ ★
Navigation:	★ ★ ★	Speed:	★ ★ ★

US

Merwan Shehariarji Irani, or Meher Baba (1894-1969) is believed by his followers to have been a manifestation of the divine in human form. The site quotes from Meher Baba, stating: 'I have come not to teach but to awaken. Understand therefore that I lay down no precepts.' Despite this, there's a useful selection of materials on the site, including messages, writings, and organisational information.

SPECIAL FEATURES

Books discusses how Meher Baba's work was 'written' and translated. Samples of Meher Baba's handwriting can be viewed.

Virtual Tour of Meher Baba's Tomb is described as a special religious experience. 'Nothing in cyberspace can replace an actual visit to Meher Baba's tomb, but this 'virtual tour' aims to give newcomers a sense of what a visit to Meherabad involves and to rekindle the experience for previous visitors. You can see photographic images of the tomb and read explanatory text and prayers.'

Meher Baba's followers have paid close attention to the internet, integrating concepts associated with religious experience into the content.

nation of yahweh

www.yahwehbenyahweh.com/
Nation of Yahweh

Overall rating: ★ ★			
Classification:	Information	Readability:	★ ★
Updating:	Occasionally	Reliability:	★ ★
Navigation:	★ ★ ★	Speed:	★ ★ ★

US

This is the official Nation of Yahweh website, depicting the work and beliefs of Yahweh ben Yahweh and his followers. Yahweh is described as 'the Great Light', and leader of the Nation, which comprises of black Hebrew Israelites. There are elements of apocalyptic theology in the pages. Although the teachings are not fully explained, there is a link to an online bookstore where further information can be obtained.

SPECIAL FEATURES

Shabbaht (sic) gives a breakdown of his beliefs, including the Nation's approach towards celebrating holy days, and details of 'persecution' suffered in the United States.

Yahweh's voice can be heard in a sequence of RealPlayer recordings. He is currently serving an 18-year sentence in Lewisburg Penitentiary in Pennsylvania for 'conspiracy' to commit racketeering. Six of his followers are also in prison serving long sentences for conspiracy.

The internet would appear to be integral to developing Yahweh's ideology, and represents an interesting example of the application of technology to promote a religious cause.

osho/rajneeshism

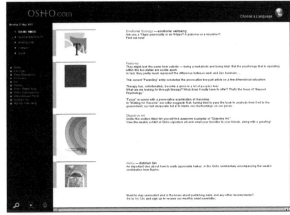

www.osho.com
Osho/Rajneeshism

Overall rating: ★ ★ ★			
Classification:	Information	**Readability:**	★ ★ ★
Updating:	Regularly	**Reliability:**	★ ★ ★
Navigation:	★ ★ ★	**Speed:**	★ ★ ★

US

Founded by Bhagwan Shree Rajneesh (1931-1990), Osho or Rajneeshism draws on their guru's hybrid influences, such as the Bible, Hindu texts, Buddhism, and meditation practices. The site is easy to navigate, and has a magazine format with a hyperlinked sidebar denoting principal categories. There are a few blank pages, but the site is much improved from earlier incarnations.

SPECIAL FEATURES

Webcasting features the No-thought of the day, in text and RealPlayer versions. Osho meditation talks can be heard on RealAudio, on themes such as: 'I want to get lost utterly and ultimately into absolute love. What should I do?', 'What is the difference between pleasure and bliss?', and 'Osho, what do you have up your sleeve?'. The Most Important Word in Our Language is Rajneesh on Nietzsche, That German Guy, and seemed to have the audience in stitches. His dialogue on 'replacement words' is more like a stand-up comedy routine, and can be experienced with RealPlayer.

Meditation features Meditation You Can Try (including Meditation of the Week). The Born Again meditation, for example, is a process that takes place for two hours a day, over seven days. For the first hour, participants take the space and freedom to behave as children. For the second hour, they sit silently, doing nothing.

OTHER FEATURES

Shop offers secure online shopping for CDs, videos and books on Osho.

This is Osho's own perspective on what is to some a controversial faith, and is classified by others as a 'cult'.

rastafarianism

www.nettilinja.fi/~hsaarist/
Rastafari Selassie Center, Finland

Overall rating: ★ ★ ★			
Classification:	Portal	Readability:	★ ★ ★
Updating:	Occasionally	Reliability:	★ ★
Navigation:	★ ★ ★	Speed:	★ ★

(FIN)

This is the northern information office of Rastafari, coordinated by Bongo Kosmo, and presenting publications in Finnish and English. The pages are splashed with photos of the site's owner, together with in-depth reasoning, and assertions such as: 'True yah, i&i no need dem catolic, orthodox, lutheran, lesbian or any kind of silvergold church. I&i are the living temples of almighty and i&i gathering on the natural way and i&i dance inna ancient yahcongo way, drumming and chanting as a natural divine ones have done so far. Rasta is the first and the last'.

SPECIAL FEATURES

Rastafari? is an explanation of the religion, containing ritual, poetry, and a discussion on reasoning.

Ital Food discusses the religious implications of diet to Rastafarians, and presents some basic recipes and drinks.

OTHER FEATURES

There are quotations from Haille Selassie drawn from diverse texts, and a specific section on Reasoning.

Slow to load, but useful as an introduction to Rastafarianism.

www.blackmind.com/Phiya/index1.html
Cyber Rasta

Overall rating: ★ ★ ★ ★			
Classification:	hformation	Readability:	★ ★ ★
Updating:	Occasionally	Reliability:	★ ★ ★
Navigation:	★ ★ ★	Speed:	★ ★

(US)

Cyber Rasta makes copious use of animation, including Bob Marley 'in action' and a Rasta bongo player touching some city riddim. As the man says: 'Jah's luv iz like phiya shut up in I bonz'. The site has a serious side, and discusses the misrepresentation of Rastafarianism by 'Babylon', and the media's tendency to stereotype Rastas by association with criminal activities. 'Once Babylon invalidates Rasta in the minds of the massive, it becomes easier to invalidate Rasta in other profound ways.' The site's main zones are indicated on the homepage.

SPECIAL FEATURES

Rastafari's Throne presents images of His Excellency Haille Selassie, the spiritual centre of the religion.

Marcus Garvey links through to a series of external sites on the preacher and social reformer.

Natty Dread Congo has some nice photos of Rastas, showing their locks and following Leviticus 19:27: 'Do not cut the hair at the sides of your head or clip off the edges of your beard.'

Rasta Chat-Bout offers live chat everyday.

Cyber Rasta is a lively site focusing on the cultural aspects of Rastafarianism.

OTHER SITES ON RASTAFARIANISM

Dread History
http://educate.si.edu/migrations/rasta
This is essentially an essay on the African Diaspora, Ethiopianism and Rastafari, which introduces key concepts and ideas surrounding the faith. There are links to a thumbnail library of various images, a bibliography, and a list of related reggae recordings.

scientology

L. Ron Hubbard was not only a best-selling science fiction author, but also the founder of the controversial Scientology Church, which has been vigorous in its use of the internet as a recruitment tool.

www.scientology.org/			
Scientology			
Overall rating: ★ ★			
Classification: Information		**Readability:**	★ ★
Updating: Regularly		**Reliability:**	★ ★
Navigation: ★ ★ ★ ★		**Speed:**	★
UK			

Presented in 11 languages, the front page contains links to the significant zones of the site, together with a search engine (on the left-hand side bar). The central menu outlines categories, including Background and Origins, Principles and Activities, and How Can Scientology Help. There are links to online Personality Tests, free information packs, and L Ron Hubbard in RealAudio. The site is easy to navigate, with a series of links at the bottom of each page directing you to the main areas of the site.

SPECIAL FEATURES

Virtual tours through Scientology Churches require QuickTime to run, and are listed according to file size and resolution preferences. Sand Hill Castle in Sussex, the UK Scientologist headquarters, can be toured in 3-D.

Glossary is an A-Z hyperlinked listing, designed to help surfers read Scientologist websites, and gives some insight into Dianetic practices.

OTHER FEATURES

FAQ should answer any basic questions about Scientology, via the searchable database. If you feel compelled to buy something, there's an online Bookstore containing Scientology publications. A Global Locator finds Scientology organisations worldwide.

This site is complex to read in places, unless you have a prior knowledge of Dianetics, or are prepared to study the pages closely.

OTHER SITES ON SCIENTOLOGY

L Ron Hubbard
www.lronhubbard.org/
This contains profiles of the Scientology Church founder, including information on his writing career, the Dianetics Letters, and Hubbard as philosopher, humanitarian, composer, and yachtsman.

transcendental meditation

www.transcendentalmeditation.org.uk/			
Transcendental Meditation			
Overall rating: ★ ★			
Classification:	Information	**Readability:**	★ ★
Updating:	Occasionally	**Reliability:**	★ ★
Navigation:	★ ★ ★ ★	**Speed:**	★ ★
UK			

Transcendental Meditation is based on Maharishi Mahesh Yogi's interpretation of Hindu Vedic Science and Technology, although its followers have been most renowned in recent years for their promotion of yogic flying during British elections through the Natural Law Party. Yogi's techniques are said to wash away stress, improve relationships, and enhance physical well-being, and are presented in detail on this site. The site is certainly relaxing to navigate: ALT labels on the left-hand side bar clearly denote the contents of hyperlinks to specific site zones.

SPECIAL FEATURES

What is TM? contains FAQs, although if you want to discuss it in more detail there is also a phone number to contact a real person. The site promotes courses in TM throughout the UK, with international links to other TM sites also available.

Scientific research justifies TM practices, with appropriate 'scientific' reference material available through hyperlinks. A printable version of the page is linked on the top of the page.

Not the most dynamic or exciting site in the world, but then you wouldn't expect that from a site about Transcendental Meditation, which is effectively an online brochure for courses.

OTHER SITES OF INTEREST

The Raelian Revolution
www.rael.org/
Can the creation myth be linked to extra-terrestrials? Is humanity the result of genetic cloning on another planet? Claude Vorilhon thought so, and wrote The Final Message to prove it, after a close encounter. The movement seeks the establishment of an Embassy in Jerusalem, to welcome visitors from other planets. Supporting evidence is provided. The material has a slow download time!

Nation of Islam
www.noi.org/
This is the official Nation of Islam homepage, full of resources and information. The pages have been running for several years, and have a professional edge to them. They also link into the Final Call newspaper, and its archives. The Honourable Minister Louis Farrakhan's Press Conferences can also be located here.

Nation of Islam Settlement No. 1
www.seventhfam.com/noilinks.htm
This links to a RealAudio archive, containing recordings of significant speeches by the founder of the Nation of Islam, Elijah Muhammad. The University of Islam link includes textual resources, such as the Qur'an, and Elijah Muhammad's books.

The Family of Love (a.k.a. The Children of God)
www.thefamily.org/
This group is often thought of in association with hippy culture. Its often controversial contents include a sound archive of the Family's founder David Berg (1919-1994), with titles including 'Fun in Heaven', 'Only God Can Do It', and 'Keep Going for God'. Provocative aspects of belief (including 'Flirty Fishing') are explained through the archive of Berg's pronouncements.

UFOs, Aliens & Antichrist: The Angelic Conspiracy & End Times Deception
www.MT.net/~watcher/
According to this site, Satan is behind UFO manifestations and the siting of aliens. The evidence is contained on this Biblically oriented site, including photos of angel debris on Mars, and cryptic clues contained in crop circles and glyphs. This site discusses end of time prophecy, and links into numerous conspiracy theory sites. The Truth is in Here?

register now at

www.thegoodwebguide.co.uk

for free updates and new website reviews

general

www.pantheon.org/mythica/
Encyclopedia Mythica

Overall rating: ★ ★ ★ ★ ★			
Classification:	Encyclopedia	Readability:	★ ★ ★ ★ ★
Updating:	Regularly	Reliability:	★ ★ ★ ★ ★
Navigation:	★ ★ ★ ★ ★	Speed:	★ ★ ★ ★ ★

NL

Encyclopedia Mythica has been online since 1995, and its author Micha F Lindemans describes it as 'an encyclopedia on mythology, folklore and legend'. The site makes excellent use of search engines, navigation tools, and site maps, to present a complex subject with informed clarity. The front page allows the surfer to explore, search, discover what's new, and find out further information about the project. Once inside the site, it can be easily navigated via the side bar available on each page.

SPECIAL FEATURES

Explore provides an entry point into the 5,700 articles featured in the Encyclopedia. Twenty-five main areas are listed, the most recent addition being Korean mythology. Each area has an A-Z directory of key terms, concepts, gods and goddesses. There are discussions on legendary places, creatures and objects from diverse religious, cultural and historical perspectives. The articles themselves have a side bar listing all the features within an area, together with links at the top of the page back to Home, Index, Search, and Feedback. Each encyclopedia entry is hyperlinked and cross-referenced, and provided with an alternative printable version.

Search is an effective engine, listing entries according to file size and relevance.

OTHER FEATURES

Folktales introduces oral and literary narratives from diverse cultural and religious perspectives. Image Gallery lists the 257 images available on the site, which are available as thumbnails, and annotated with file size.

Encyclopedia Mythica is a state-of-the-art resource with a broad worldview, which presents mythology with an informed clarity and accessibility.

mythology, pantheism, polytheism and the spirit world

african related religions

The internet is a great place to discover more about religions (outside of Christianity and Islam) that have their roots in African cultures and traditions. Like the web, many of these beliefs transcend continents and have amazing networking connections with one another.

http://isizoh.net/afrel/			
African Traditional Religions			
Overall rating: ★ ★ ★ ★			
Classification:	Information	**Readability:**	★ ★ ★
Updating:	Regularly	**Reliability:**	★ ★ ★ ★
Navigation:	★ ★ ★ ★	**Speed:**	★ ★ ★
NIG			

This is a scholarly site produced by Chidi Denis Isizoh, with much of interest to the general surfer. The diversity of African traditional religious expression is well represented on the links contained on this site, together with its original content. The front page links into all the zones on the site, under the titles of Topical Issues, Introduction to Aspects of Religion, Meeting Points on the Three Great Religions in Africa, and Practice of African Traditional Religion.

SPECIAL FEATURES

Topical Issues is a useful archive of essays, with titles ranging from Creation in African Thought through to the Role of Women in African Traditional Religion.

Official voice of the Catholic Church on African Traditional Religion and Cultural Values describes papal attitudes and official papers.

Practice of African Religion links into important external sites relating to Orisha, Voodoo, and Candomblé practices.

OTHER FEATURES

Targeted Links and **Other Good Links** offer a fascinating selection of material, including details of Yoruba faith and other forms of religion in Africa, South and Central America and the Caribbean.

This is an excellent portal representing some of the diversity of faith in sub-Saharan Africa.

OTHER SITES

Africana: African Religions: An Interpretation
www.africana.com/tt_349.htm
This article is taken from Africana, which is a useful African-American-centred encyclopedia. There is a discussion on western interpretations of African religions, notions of supreme beings, the spirit world, and forms of religious expression. A few associated hyperlinks would have improved the article, but it is certainly required reading for anyone interested in the complex and diverse forms of African faith.

Call of the Drums

altreligion.about.com/religion/altreligion/library/weekly/
aa041400a.htm
This is an interesting hyperlinked essay, discussing African-Caribbean beliefs, and their links with slavery. There are links to pages on Voodoo, Santeria, and Candomblé.

Santera/Yoruba

West African/Yoruba origin practices travelled to the Americas and the Caribbean, and are detailed on these pages.

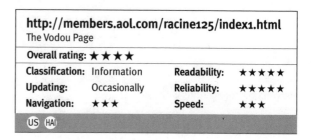

http://members.aol.com/racine125/index1.html
The Vodou Page

Overall rating: ★ ★ ★ ★			
Classification: Information		**Readability:**	★ ★ ★ ★ ★
Updating: Occasionally		**Reliability:**	★ ★ ★ ★ ★
Navigation: ★ ★ ★		**Speed:**	★ ★ ★

US HAI

This is a very useful link page to Vodou (voodoo) practices, written by a Mambo priestess, Mambo Racine, who was initiated in Haiti. The front page links to the site's main areas, including Lessons, Vodou and Haitian Politics, and Writings by Women in African-Caribbean Traditions.

SPECIAL FEATURES

Vodou Lessons are open to all, and richly illustrated. As well as providing religious and historical backgrounds to vodou, the section offers advice on getting started, including Constructing an Altar, Making an Ancestral Feast, and A Mambo's Experience.

Special Topics has sections on religion and magic, possession, and a few Vodou jokes. The page on sexuality confronts stereotypes, and discusses wanga, or spells, for love.

Vodou Initiation discusses ritual, offers participation in initiation groups, and links to a good external site on the initiation cycle. One link on this section was broken.

Greetings in the name of God Goddess, the ancestors, and the lwa!

Mwen salwe tout peti Gines caso Kendre ak Sof lwa yo!

My name is Bon Mambo Racine Sans Bout Sa Te La Daginen, "Roots Without End, Who Was Already There, of Guinea". Mambo Racine for short. I am a Mambo, an initiated and ordained priestess of Haitian Vodou. I was initiated as Mambo asogwe in July 1999, in Grand Goave in the north of Haiti, by Mambo Lili Dudette, Sou Houngan Jaclike Halbeau, "Good Houngan Step Over Evil", houngan to him! I received my vows in August of 1999 in an outlying district of Jacmel in Haiti's southern coast, with Mapoune Dayisé David, Yabofe Bon Houngan, honor to him!

The Vodou tradition is a rich and complex one, and I invite you to begin your exploration! As a Mambo, I am competent to speak on Vodou. I have spoken at colleges and universities in the United States, and appeared on "The Learning Channel". I am capable of performing correct, authentic initiation ceremonies, and I am also competent to do divination (readings), work charms, prescribe herbal baths, and assist people to construct altars, make food offerings, and other ritual activities. I am able to lead Vodou ceremonies.

If you would like to discuss issues pertaining to this religion or to my ability to assist people in the attainment of their objectives, drop me a line and let's talk!

Farther down this page you will find:

New Links!
The Vodou Lessons
Special Topics
Initiation in Haitian Vodou
Vodou and Haitian Politics
Writings by Women in Afro-Caribbean Traditions
Links to Sites on Vodou and Related Traditions

Mambo Racine Sans Bout exchanges ceremonial gestures with Houngan Luc

OTHER FEATURES

The site is richly illustrated by photos, which took some time to download. It contains some great links to other sites, and interactive opportunities via chat rooms. There is a section on vodou's spelling. The Vodou Emporium offers genuine ritual materials by email order/letter (no secure shopping).

The Vodou Page is a very accessible site, which presents rich resources on cultural and religious aspects of vodou.

www.church-of-the-lukumi.org/
Church of the Lukumi Babalu Aye

Overall rating: ★ ★ ★			
Classification:	Information	Readability:	★ ★ ★
Updating:	Occasionally	Reliability:	★ ★ ★
Navigation:		Speed:	★ ★

US CUB

This is an 'academic resource', in Spanish and English, which seeks to address misconceptions about the religion, which it defines as 'Yoruba' (from Nigeria) rather than 'Santeiri'. The site also discusses the repression of its members in Cuba under Castro. Scroll down the front pageand click the Enter English link to come to the Table of Contents.

SPECIAL FEATURES

CBLA Journal contains detailed and well-referenced articles. For example, see the article on Syncretism by Oba Ernesto Pichardo (in Contemporary), and the article on Thrones Of The Orishas by David Brown (in Art and Culture).

Consultation offers a Cyber Spiritual Service, using traditional methods of confession and divination. A charge of US $30 is levied.

OTHER FEATURES

The site contains a bookstore, and accepts online orders, although you have to send your money order by snail mail.

The Church of the Lukumi Babalu Aye have an informed site on an under-represented subject, which makes for fascinating reading on diverse Yoruba religious and cultural practices.

OTHER SITES

OrishaNet

www.seanet.com/~efunmoyiwa/ochanet.html

Controversy regarding animal sacrifices has surrounded the religion, and 'misconceptions' about this are answered on Orisha Net. There is information about traditional consultation with shells (not available over the net), under the heading For If· and Merindilogún (Shells) Consultations. Some interesting articles are available on the site, such as 'The Religion In Africa and Cuba: How Different Are They Really?', and the Legends of the Orishas.

native american

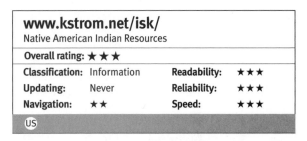

www.kstrom.net/isk/			
Native American Indian Resources			
Overall rating: ★ ★ ★			
Classification:	Information	**Readability:**	★★★
Updating:	Never	**Reliability:**	★★★
Navigation:	★★	**Speed:**	★★★
US			

This fascinating resource links to hundreds of pages, including rich information about Native American faith practices. Unfortunately, the site's author died in 1997, but the pages have been maintained in her memory and its content is still valid. An overhaul of the site started in 2000, to repair broken links. Scroll down the main page to explore the various sections, as at present there is no search engine.

Native Astronomy presents the stars from a Native American perspective, including an impressive array of links to academic and/or Native American material. It includes sources facilitating the evaluation of star positions for prayer and ceremonies.

Aadizookaanag contains various legends and myths, including sacred material, from diverse tribes incorporated under the Native American banner.

Manidoominens are Spirit Seeds, and are described here in religious, cultural and historical contexts.

Unique perspectives on Native American worldviews are available here, on a site that deserves further tender loving care.

OTHER SITES

Beothuk Religious Practices
www.mun.ca/rels/native/
Native American religious practices, as found in Newfoundland and Labrador.

Seminoles and Christianity
www.seminoletribe.com/culture/christianity.shtml
Florida tribes present their story of the coming of Christianity to their cultures.

pantheist/polytheist

While it is not possible to represent here the incredible diversity of pantheistic and polytheistic views available online (outside of the excellent Encyclopedia Mythica), the following brief listing contains some recommended starting points of areas of polytheism/pantheism not covered elsewhere in this book. Many contain photos and historical information, and in some cases there are indications of the contemporary beliefs associated with these faiths.

Ancient Egypt

Egyptian Myths
www.egyptianmyths.com/

Australian Aboriginal

Lore of the Land
www.loreoftheland.com.au/

National Aboriginal and Torres Straits Islander Education Website
www.natsiew.nexus.edu.au/lens/

Greek

Myth Man
http://mythman.com/

Korea

Myths and Legends of Ancient Korea
http://violet.berkeley.edu/~korea/legends.html

Maori

Maori Organisations of New Zealand
www.maori.org.nz/

Mesopotamia and Babylon

Gateways to Babylon
www.angelfire.com/tx/gatestobabylon/

Polynesian

Polynesian Culture
www.iaora.com/NatHist/polynesian_culture.htm

Roman

A Roman Pantheon
http://web.raex.com/~obsidian/RomPan.html

Scandanavia

Nordic Mythology
www.luth.se/luth/present/sweden/history/gods/
Old_norse_myth.html

esoteric and new age

new age

The term 'New Age' can cover a multitude of approaches to faith, often with perceived historical roots dating back to ancient practices. The extent to which the term represents 'religion' is probably up to the individual. For many people, these practices are central to their worldviews.

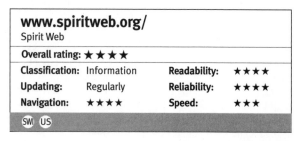

www.spiritweb.org/
Spirit Web

Overall rating: ★ ★ ★ ★			
Classification:	Information	**Readability:**	★ ★ ★ ★
Updating:	Regularly	**Reliability:**	★ ★ ★ ★
Navigation:	★ ★ ★ ★	**Speed:**	★ ★ ★

SWI US

Spirit Web has an outlook on what it describes as 'alternative approaches to spirituality, besides the established religions'. The New Age feel to the content should not dissuade those seeking to surf different approaches to faith. The front page has a magazine format, with information on the most recent original articles, many of a mystical nature. Typical titles include 'How are you using your cosmic resources?', 'Fine-tuning your spiritual awareness', and 'Understanding Vibrational Rhythms'. Primary zones are listed on the left-hand side bar, which also contains a search engine.

SPECIAL FEATURES

Reincarnation contains a series of articles representing different worldviews to soul-evolution, karma, and near-death experience. It also offers classic thoughts on the subject, ranging from the Egyptian Book of the Dead to the Kabbalah.

Yoga defines different paths and schools of the ancient teachings, with descriptions and links to original Spirit Web articles and external sites. This is the most comprehensive link page on yoga in relation to faith that we have found on the web.

OTHER FEATURES

For those people for whom faith incorporates elements of Mysticism, Astrology, Healing, and Out of Body experiences, Spirit Web offers an ideal source of online knowledge and experience with dedicated, quality pages in these areas. Web chat, mailing lists and membership are available. There is also a shop, with secure online ordering.

The site has been online since 1994, and this experience shows in a well-informed and professional browsing experience about alternative faith.

neopagan

Australian Vampire Information Association (AVIA)
www.avia.darkrealm.net/
From Transylvania to Tasmania, vampires now have a stake on the web on this nicely organised site, under the motto 'Get a Life. Get Undead'. AVIA features a newsletter entitled Bloodlines, vampire products, a message board, and links to other vampire-related material: 'Whether you are a vampire, lead a vampiric lifestyle, are a vampirologist, have been attacked by a vampire (either physically or psychically), or are simply interested, AVIA can be of benefit to you.'

Avatarsearch
www.avatarsearch.com/
Avatarsearch is the premier place to start exploring aspects of neo-paganism. It describes itself as the 'search engine of the occult internet', and is regularly updated, with select links of the month, links to occult online stores, and a calendar of significant occult events. Avatar organises an Occult Dating service (not tested by this writer). Note that each hyperlink will take you to a new window. The side bar includes a link to switch off frames.

Nightstorms Coven
http://nightstorms.tripod.com/
The purple/pink text on black sets the tone for this spellbinding mystical journey into Wiccan/witchcraft beliefs, which is loaded with detailed information about the coven. 'Nightstorms is directly descended from the Isle of Shadow Coven of the Warrior/Goddess Scathach of 300 A.D. Ireland, where the members of the Order of the Red Branch were trained by the Goddess herself.' The main page lists areas of interest, including various rituals, sex and magic, and a guide to the 'beliefs and superstitions surrounding witchcraft'. They also get to dress up a lot.

Pagan Path

www.paganpath.com

Pagan Path contains a wealth of original material for pagans, witches and Wiccans. The clarity of this site comes as a relief, especially the easy-to-navigate articles. Find out what a witch should have in the garden, the use of altars in magic, the 13 principles of the Wiccan belief (as approved by the US Army), and read advice on psychics and divination. There is a substantial section of love spells (but no guarantees). Elsewhere on the Pagan Path, there's an online shop, which despite the Dragon's Blood Box claims that none of the merchandise contains animal products. Secure ordering by credit card is available. Even the uninitiated will find the site interesting.

Shamanism

http://deoxy.org/shaman.htm

This is an introductory listing of shamanism resources, appropriately chaotic in places, but containing substantial information on a variety of practices, primarily associated with North and South America. Hyperlinks do not always indicate whether a sound file, message board, or other data is about to be downloaded. The technological and psychedelic elements of this worldview are probably of most interest to existing shamans. Search engines lead to other specialist areas.

Witches' Voice

www.witchvox.com/

The Witches' Voice has a five-year track record of providing news and information, and now includes Spanish, Finnish, Italian and Latvian sections. For beginners, the FAQs, 'So you wanna be a witch', and articles on cats, Magick, pagan holidays and practices should be of interest. 'The Witches' Voice is a proactive educational network dedicated to correcting misinformation about witches and witchcraft. Witchcraft – Wicca IS a legally recognized religion in the United States and it is our mission to protect that right through education and awareness.' So there.

celtic religion and druidry

Celtic Religion takes many forms, and on the web is linked into a variety of subject interests relating to beliefs and spirituality, including 'magic', the occult, paganism, poetry, and religious history. Not all of those practitioners would necessarily wish to be linked into these interests! There are hundreds of sites relating to Celtic Religion, Druid and associated beliefs. The following are useful entry points.

www.keltria.org/			
Henge of Keltria			
Overall rating: ★ ★ ★			
Classification:	Information	Readability:	★ ★ ★
Updating:	Regularly	Reliability:	★ ★ ★
Navigation:	★ ★ ★	Speed:	★ ★ ★ ★
US			

Henge of Keltria is a 'positive path neopagan tradition dedicated to protecting and preserving our Mother Earth, honouring our ancestors, revering the spirits of nature, and worshipping the gods and goddesses of our Celtic heritage'. The main page is easy to navigate, either through the top bar or by scrolling down the page. The site contains a journal, and membership (not required to surf the site).

SPECIAL FEATURES

What is Henge of Keltria? introduces the initiatory tradition, in which 'rings' measure participants' attainments. There is information defining neo-paganism and druidism, answering FAQs about sacrifice and the building of Stonehenge.

A developed resource on Celtic Magick and Druidism, with opportunities for interactivity.

www.imbas.org/
IMBAS

Overall rating: ★ ★ ★			
Classification:	Information	Readability:	★ ★ ★
Updating:	Regularly	Reliability:	★ ★ ★
Navigation:	★ ★ ★	Speed:	★ ★ ★

US

IMBAS (pronounced 'im-bus') is an Old Irish word meaning 'poetic inspiration'. IMBAS exists to promote the religion of Celtic Reconstructionist Paganism and the cultural heritage of the Celtic peoples.

Celtic Reconstructionist Paganism would seem to have several definitions. The IMBAS perspective presented here includes a discussion on animal symbolism, Celtic deities, and Celtic law. The site opens with the symbols for Celtic triads. Clicking on the symbol takes you to an explanation about IMBAS, and a site map. The site could benefit from an effective search engine.

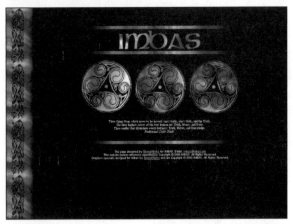

SPECIAL FEATURES

Foclóir Draíochta or Dictionary of Druidism, is a text-only listing of Druid terminology, which reveals a great deal about the belief system. There are hundreds of entries, from abhainn to urnaidhm.

Druidism FAQ takes you to a hyperlinked book, 'The Solitary Practitioner's Basic Guide to the Druids and Celtic Mysticism'. History, customs, contemporary traditions, and expressions of spirit are all covered in detail.

An Essay on Sacrifice outlines the pros and cons of cosmological sacrifice, whether animal or herbal.

OTHER FEATURES

Some of the material here has an academic orientation, such as the An Tríbhís Mhór journal. Celtic religious books can be purchased via Amazon.com, and the Internet Bookshop (separate pages).

IMBAS is naturally specialist in nature, but there's also plenty of introductory information and curiosities for the casual surfer.

www.geocities.com/RainForest/1669/			
Druidry			
Overall rating: ★ ★			
Classification:	Homepage	**Readability:**	★ ★
Updating:	Occasionally	**Reliability:**	★ ★
Navigation:	★ ★ ★	**Speed:**	★ ★ ★
US			

Tribal Gaels, living in North Carolina, had fun putting graphics, animation and unusual fonts onto this site, which won't win any design awards but is nevertheless entertaining. Navigate via the grid at the bottom of the front page. They confront the reader with numerous questions: What does the word 'Druid' really mean? What exactly did the 'Druids' do? What is Magic? Is there such a thing as Black and/or White Magic? Did the 'Druids' perform sacrifice? Is a 'Druid' the same as a Wiccan? What is the difference between a neo-pagan practitioner and someone who pursues the scholarly side of Gaelic/Celtic culture? Am I a 'Druid'?

SPECIAL FEATURES

Rampant Lion attempts to provide answers to these questions on this page, which also contains academic quotations and background information to Druidry presented by Tribal Gaels.

This virtual tour of Druidry is a lively set of introductory resources, with plenty of links for further reading.

OTHER SITES

Order of Bards, Ovates and Druids
http://druidry.org/
A sequence of interactive pages take the reader through symbols and poems relating to Druidism, accompanied by appropriate music. The site provides information on Druid origins, festivals, initiations, and a course to facilitate moving through the Druid ranks.

want to read **more reviews** on this subject?
log on to **www.thegoodwebguide.co.uk**

esoteric dimensions of religion

Many of the esoteric dimensions of religion have been introduced in the Guide's sections on World Religions, Other Beliefs, and Categories and Concepts. The following sites incorporate other aspects of mystical knowledge, from diverse faith perspectives.

www.elib.com/Steiner/
Rudolf Steiner Archive

Overall rating: ★ ★ ★ ★			
Classification:	Library	Readability:	★ ★ ★
Updating:	Regularly	Reliability:	★ ★ ★ ★
Navigation:	★ ★ ★	Speed:	★ ★ ★

UK

Rudolf Steiner (1861-1925) developed the 'science of the spirit', or anthroposophy. His work has been influential in the development of theosophy and related beliefs.

SPECIAL FEATURES

E-Library offers electronic versions of Steiner's work, from his published writings through to more obscure material. Many significant titles are available to download, to read on or offline.

Those with a taste for mysticism and esoteric perspectives of faith will find much of interest within this important resource.

www.blavatsky.net/
Blavatsky Net

Overall rating: ★ ★ ★			
Classification:	Portal	Readability:	★ ★ ★
Updating:	Regularly	Reliability:	★ ★ ★
Navigation:	★ ★ ★	Speed:	★ ★ ★ ★

US

This site focuses on Madame Blavatsky (1831-91) and her teaching of theosophy ('Divine Knowledge'). It features an introduction to theosophy, study aids, original text of theosophy, supporting evidence, membership, and visitor interaction. The main page of the site also acts as a useful link page to other sites containing theosophy-related material.

SPECIAL FEATURES

Basic Principles is a succinct one-page introduction to theosophy, indicating some of the influences on this belief system.

Blavatsky Text Online offers the essential texts, such as Secret Doctrine (on the creation of the universe), Isis Unveiled (esoteric teachings), and the introductory Key to Theosophy.

OTHER FEATURES

Roadmap delineates the cyber routes towards theosophy. Bookstore offers secure credit card ordering.

There are a number of perspectives surrounding theosophy, and this is a useful entry point, although some of the content is definitely for specialists.

www.oversoul.org/
Oversoul

Overall rating: ★★			
Classification:	Information	**Readability:**	★★★
Updating:	Occasionally	**Reliability:**	★★
Navigation:	★★★	**Speed:**	★★★

US

The front page explains the term 'oversoul', which is associated with Ralph Waldo Emerson's term, meaning 'over abiding presence'.

SPECIAL FEATURES

Articles includes titles such as New Consciousness and Spirituality, Laws of Nature, and Nature and the Biosphere.

OTHER FEATURES

For some reason, loading the site resulted in persistent piano music being played, which couldn't be turned off. While reading about spiritual healing requests, healing pets, and developing medium ship, readers might look out for a cure to errant sound files.

When technical problems are healed, Oversoul will be an easier read of an interesting subject.

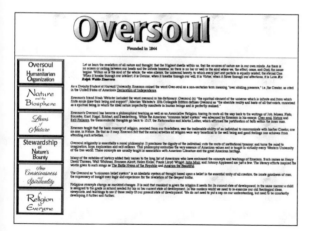

other esoteric resources

www.digiserve.com/mystic/
Mysticism in World Religions

Overall rating: ★ ★ ★ ★ ★			
Classification:	Library/Homepage	Readability:	★ ★ ★ ★
Updating:	Regularly	Reliability:	★ ★ ★ ★ ★
Navigation:	★ ★ ★ ★	Speed:	★ ★ ★ ★ ★

US

This is an impressive collection of material relating to different mystical world views from six world religions, including quotations from key texts and a glossary of terms. Cross-referenced, the site is organised by topics, themes, and religions. This is a great starting point for exploration of the esoteric dimensions of faith.

SPECIAL FEATURES

The Short List provides an illustrative quotation from every page on the site, providing an overview of content, and avenues for further exploration.

Focus on One Religion accesses all the site content available on Judaism, Christianity, Islam, Hinduism, Buddhism or Taoism.

OTHER FEATURES

Mystics, Theologians and Scriptures allows the reader to discover all the content from a particular mystic, regardless of topic. Quotations from World Religions is a thematic listing of important mystical questions, such as Dying and Being Reborn and Distinguishing Ego from True Self.

An accessible encyclopedia of mysticism, discussing approaches from diverse world views.

OTHER SITES

Mysticism Resources
www.clas.ufl.edu/users/gthursby/mys/
This is a link page, highlighting different approaches towards mysticism in world religions. There are useful sections on Mysticisms from the Middle East, Mysticisms from Asia, Native American Spiritualities, and Prayer and Meditation.

Chapter 04

contexts and categories

This chapter offers a comparative approach to looking at religions using the internet. You may wish to call up several of the pages listed in each section simultaneously.

Some sections in this chapter bring together the diverse religions of the world, and explore their connectivity and inter-relationship, as well as their differences, through different religious phenomena. There are many ideas on the internet surrounding what is 'sacred'. For example, Sacred Language demonstrates the different prayers and invocations available though the net (often in audio format). Sacred Places introduces notions surrounding pilgrimage, and its online manifestations, including the suggestion that it might be possible to undertake religious obligations to 'visit' sacred places through the internet. Religious People presents historical and contemporary religious influences and leaders, which have had some impact on the development of the religions of the world. Online Authority shows that use of the internet means that religious authorities and intermediaries can be contacted via email, and this has implications for the nature of traditional authority and the structure of religions, as well as the breadth of issues which now have to be tackled by authorities, whether they are 'official' or (in some cases) self-appointed. Sacred and Religious Concepts brings together the phenomena which are shared between religions, so that they can be compared and contrasted. Sacred Texts indicates the importance of digital sources as a means to learn about religion, and that their searchable qualities can add much to reading even the most familiar text. Some would suggest that there is much to learn from other religious beliefs, and that there can be a commonality of religious experience between diverse traditions.

Other sections in this chapter illustrate the contemporary and, at times, controversial qualities of world religions and their expression on the internet. Science and Religion demonstrates the ways in which the question of how religion can be reconciled with science is being dealt with. Be prepared for lively dialogue, as well as resources which illustrate that there are at least two sides to every story. The combination of Religion, Gender and Sexuality can be provocative, especially to some religious traditionalists; the internet provides one way in which marginalised or disenfranchised people can dialogue in safety (applying anonymity if required) while retaining their religious beliefs.

The cultural and social dimensions of religion also have a place on the internet, and provide various forms of sustenance, religious experience, and in some cases entertainment. Sacred Food highlights the ritualistic significance of food and drink, whilst directing the reader towards nutritious and informative websites. Despite the fact that the technology prohibits a culinary experience being immediately acquired via the internet, the suggested sites provide the means for creating or obtaining religiously oriented food. To heighten the quality of your surfing, an appropriate soundtrack can be obtained through the Sacred Sounds section, where an incredible selection of music can be obtained. Whether you wish to chill out or be spiritually uplifted, there is something there for most musical tastes. If the content of some sites has become too serious for you, then try the Humour section of this chapter. The quality of some of the material may not make you laugh out loud, but it is interesting what some people find amusing. Religion can be a rich source of humour, and many important religious figures have stressed the need (or duty) to laugh.

Further Surfing offers leads into other areas of cyberspace, primarily academic in orientation, which may answer questions that cannot be solved through other sites listed in this Guide.

sacred and religious concepts

This is an overview of selected sacred concepts that can be found on the internet, although a full listing would require a separate encyclopedia-sized volume. These concepts illustrate a rich complexity of approaches to faith, ranging from practices whose history dates back thousands of years, through to recent innovations such as the Toronto Blessing. All are introduced online, often with opportunities for personal participation or education to fulfil a sacred objective. Links listed here usually take surfers directly to specific pages relating to a sacred concept. Rating a concept is unnecessary in the eye of the beholder, for whom the sacred cannot always be quantified or rationalised. However, these are some of the most interesting faith-related pages on the internet.

angels

Angels in Judaism
www.beth-elsa.org/be_s1212.htm

Catholics Online
http://saints.catholic.org/angels.html

Open Directory: Angels
http://dmoz.org/Society/Religion_and_Spirituality/
Christianity/Topics/Angels/

Simply Islam: Angels
http://tariq.bitshop.com/simplyIslam/angels.htm

Study of Angels and the Dimensions
www.spiritweb.org/Spirit/angelic-realms.html

Yazdânism or Cult of Angels
www.humanrights.de/~kurdweb/kwd/english/society/
religion/cult.html

dharma

Hindu Web
www.hinduweb.org

Spirit Web
www.spiritweb.org/Spirit/veda.html

divination

Church of the Lukumi
www.church-of-the-lukumi.org/

Day of the Dead
www.peoplesguide.com/1pages/chapts/viva/dodead/
1dodindex.html

Divination Tools and Supplies
www.maxinet.com/shadows/divin.htm

Druid Ritual
http://druidry.org/

Magick and Divination
http://209.52.189.2/welcome.cfm/magick_and_divination

exorcism

Christian

Ancient Christian
http://ccat.sas.upenn.edu/~humm/Courses/Demons/Res
ources/liturgy.html

Catholic
www.newadvent.org/cathen/05709a.htm
www.stmichael.pair.com/

Christianity in Sri Lanka
www.evaldon.com/christian/RENOUNCE.html

Jewish

Exorcism by Rabbis
http://faculty.biu.ac.il/~barilm/exorcism.html

Miscellaneous

Fortean Times
www.forteantimes.com/artic/123/exoextra.html

Occult Perspective
www.themystica.com/mystica/articles/e/exorcism.html

Muslim

Five Pillars of Islam
http://oak.cats.ohiou.edu/~muslimst/islam/islam5.html

Ibn Taymeeyah's Essay On The Jinn (Demons)
www.islaam.com/bp/jinn2.htm

Interviews with Muslim Exorcists
www.angelfire.com/al/islamicpsychology/exorcism.html

The World of the Jinn
www.calltoislaam.free-online.co.uk/articles/the_world_of_the_jinn.html

genealogy

Church of the Latter Day Saints
www.lds.org

healing

Spirit Web
www.spiritweb.org/Spirit/healing.html

Christian
www.stmichael.pair.com/HEALINGS.htm

Jewish

Jewish Healing Perspectives
http://web.wt.net/~cbenton/healing/heal.htm

Kabbalah Healing
http://kabbalah.org/

Shamanic Healing
http://bayarea.net/~stef/shamanism/whatissham.html

Muslim

Physical and Spiritual Health: Protection and Healing From an Islamic Perspective
http://oak.cats.ohiou.edu/~aa237291/spirit.html

heaven/afterlife

Jannah (Paradise)
www.jannah.org/articles/treeofiman.html

Olam Ha-Ba: The Afterlife Judaism 101
www.jewfaq.org/olamhaba.htm

Near Death Experiences
www.near-death.com/

Welcome to a Heavenly Revelation
www.she.org/Heaven/index.htm

Predestination

Hindunet
www.hindunet.org/alt_hindu/1995_Mar_2/msg00081.html

holy spirit

Christian Keys
http://homepages.go.com/~christiankeys/HolySpirit.html

Examining the Scriptures
http://edge.edge.net/~paul101/trinity.htm

Novena to the Holy Spirit
www.immaculateheart.com/Mary/html/holy_spirit.htm

ikons

Digital Coptic Stuff
http://church.salib.com/

Ethiopian Orthodox Tewahedo Church (EOTC)
www.students.uiuc.edu/~moges/orth.html

Russian Icons
www.auburn.edu/academic/liberal_arts/foreign/russian/
icons/index.html

kabbalah

A Gateway to the Wisdom of Kabbalah and Chassidut
www.inner.org/

Kabbalah
http://aish.com/spirituality/kabbala101/Kabbala_1_-
_What_Is_Kabbala$.asp

karma and reincarnation

members.home.net/lumiere/karma/mystknow.htm

kirpan

www.sikhs.org

lingam

Society of Heaven and Earth
www.she.org/pw/hindu.htm

miracles

www.mcn.org/1/miracles/

mysteria (mysterium)

Mysterium Online (German language)
www.usm.de/mysteria/mysteria.htm

nirvana

www.geocities.com/Tokyo/5215/

prophecy

Greater Things
www.greaterthings.com/Visions/

**Predictions for 2000-2007 of world events, by Astrology
and New Age Analysis**
http://homepages.go.com/~tomchase/tomchase.html

Prophetic Dreams
www.angelfire.com/ms/mydream/

reincarnation

Buddhism's View on The Wheel of Rebirth
www.ibps.org/english/master/wheel of rebirth.html

Phenomena of Death by L. Ron Hubbard (Scientology)
www.ronthephilosopher.org/page62.htm

Reincarnation and Karma in the Bible
http://inetport.com/~one/rnkbib.html

Sacred Flame – Zarathushtra
www.zarathushtra.com

Shroud of Turin
www.shroud.com/

SpiritWeb
www.spiritweb.org/Spirit/reincarnation.html

Star of David – Judaism 101
www.jewfaq.org

The Tradition of Reincarnation (Vajrayana)
www.tibet.dk/tsurphu/karmapa/traditio.html

sacrifice

Henge of Keltria
www.keltria.org

OrishaNet
www.seanet.com~e/unmoyiwa/ochanet.html

Qurbani
www.islaam.org/Qurbaani/qurba-con.htm

sufism

Javanese Mysticism
www.xs4all.nl/~wichm/javmys1.html

Sufism's Many Paths
www.arches.uga.edu/~godlas/Sufism.html

Torat-Chayim
www.jtsa.edu/lists/tor-ch/

ultimate reality

99 Perfect Names and Attributes of Allah
www.geocities.com/Athens/Academy/7368/islam_99_na
mes.htm

The Most Beautiful Names of Allah
http://islam.org/mosque/99names.htm

House of Yahweh
www.yahweh.com

Mission to Israel
www.missiontoisrael.org/sacred-name.html

The Catholic Encyclopedia
www.newadvent.org/cathen/08329a.htm

The Truth of Yahweh – A Biblical Review
www.goodnet.com/~shem/

Yogic Flying
www.yogic-flying.org

miscellaneous

Art & Aums
www.himalayanacademy.com/art/aum/display.htm/

Doctrines of Grace (Reformed Evangelical Christians)
www.grace.org.uk/faith/index.html

Dakhma-nashini (Zoroastrian Funeral Rite)
www.ozemail.com.au/~zarathus/tenets33.html

Toronto Blessing – Toronto Airport Christian Facility
www.tacf.org/

sacred language: prayer and invocation

As can be seen on many of the sites discussed elsewhere in this Guide, religion can be expressed in many forms. This section is designed to be a user-friendly listing of prayer and invocation from a variety of faith perspectives. Transcending fixed categories, this listing demonstrates that there is a lot of common ground between diverse religious perspectives. RealPlayer and Windows Media Player (or equivalent) may be required, in order to experience the sounds (and visions) of sacred language.

prayer

Anglican Catholic liturgy and sermons
www.anglicancatholic.org

Benedictine Psalms and Readings: Benedictine Network
www.benedictine.net/

Benny Hinn Ministries
www.bennyhinn.org/

Buddhist Chanting
www.buddhanet.net/bn_rachant.htm

Carmel Carmelite Nuns
www.pressenter.com/~carmelit/

Catholic Information Network
www.cin.org

Celtic Prayers – IMBAS
www.imbas.org/

Church of the Brethren Network
www.cob-net.org/inform.htm

Church of England liturgy
www.cofe.anglican.org

Coptic Devotional Material
www.frugal.com/~stmary/Agpeya.html

CyberSalat (Muslim prayer)
www.ummah.net/software/cyber

Fatima Network
www.fatima.org/

First Church of Cyberspace
www.godweb.org/index1.html

Hare Krishna
www.webcom.com/ara/col/books/BIO/prab.html

Jesus Army Prayer
www.jesus.org.uk/

Jewish Prayers – Aish HaTorah
http://aish.com

Mantra On Net
www.mantraonnet.com/

Mass – When to Kneel, Stand or Sit at Low, High, Requiem or Solemn Mass
www.netacc.net/~bbasile/stsk.htm

Meditation – Cyber Monks
www.teleport.com/~interlud/

Mosque of the Internet
www.mosque.com

Oremus Daily Christian Prayer
www.oremus.org

Orthodox Christian Resources on the Internet
www.hrweb.org/orthodox/

Orthodox Church of Antioch in Great Britain
www.antiochian-orthodox.co.uk/indexnj.html

Protestant Hour
www.protestanthour.com/

Shiva Darshan
www.charm.net/~nayak/shiva.html

Sikh Network
www.sikhnet.com

**Syrian Orthodox Lord's Prayer (Abun d'Bashmayocan) –
Syrian Orthodox Resources**
www.netadventure.com/~soc/

The Divya Prabandham
www.ramanuja.org/sv/prabandham/index.html

World Puja
www.worldpuja.org/

Zoroastrian Liturgy
www.avesta.org

invocation

Christian
www.chrysostom.org/andrew/verse/invocation.html
www.catholic-forum.com/saints/prayo112.htm

Enochian
www.crl.com/~tzimon/Workings/epbr.html

Humanist
http://humanist.net/ceremonies/invocation-1.html

Jewish
www.digiserve.com/mystic/Jewish/Scholem_1/mantra.html

Muslim
www.digiserve.com/mystic/Muslim/Ibn_Ata_Allah/mantra.html
www.digiserve.com/mystic/Muslim/Rumi/mantra.html
http://al-islam1.org/nahjul/letters/letter15.htm

New Age
www.spiritweb.org/Spirit/invocations.html
www.lucistrust.org/invocation/

Order of the Thelemic Golden Dawn.
www.pagans.org/~firerose/invocati.htm

Parthian
www.webcom.com/~gnosis/library/invocgod.htm

Vedic
www.anandaashram.org/Sanskrit/peace.html

Yoga
www.itsyoga.com/manual/invocation.html

sacred places

What makes a place sacred? Temples, shrines, churches, synagogues, gurdawara, and pilgrimage sites can all be classified as sacred places. This is a route map of their manifestations in cyberspace, for those seeking out sacred places, although some would say that such travel is unnecessary in order to locate the sacred within an individual. Sites listed here range from simple homepages containing a few pictures, to sophisticated cyber tours. They give an indication of the different forms sacred places can take, and of the individual devotion, enthusiasm and, in some cases, hardship that surrounds a ritual visit.

allahabad

Channel 4 – Kumbh Mela
www.channel4.co.uk/kumbhmela/

avebury

Earth Mysteries: Avebury
http://witcombe.sbc.edu/earthmysteries/EMAvebury.html

bodhgaya

www.investindia.com/DIWebzine2/bodhgaya.htm

canterbury cathedral

www.canterbury-cathedral.org/

constantinople

Greek Orthodox Diocese of America
www.goarch.org/

egyptian temples:

Karnak
www.eyelid.co.uk/karnak1.htm

Luxor/Thebes
www.powerup.com.au/~ancient/luxor.htm

Thebes Photographic Project
www-oi.uchicago.edu/OI/TVE_TPP/TVE_TPP.html

hagia sofia

www.focusmm.com.au/civilization/hagia/welcome.htm

iona

www.iona.org.uk/

jerusalem

Al Quds (Islam)
www.ummah.net/sanders

Via Dolorosa (Christianity)
www.christusrex.org/www1/ofm/melita.html

Western Wall (Judaism)
http://aish.com/

kabah, mecca

www.islam.org

lindisfarne

www.lindisfarne.org.uk/

madurai

www.madurai.com/

megalithic sites and mounds
http://witcombe.sbc.edu/earthmysteries/EMMegaSites.html

meher baba's tomb
www.AvatarMeherBaba.org/tomb.html

mount fuji
www.primenet.com/%7Emartman/ns.html

sabari
www.hindu.dk

sacred space in viking law and religion
www.realtime.com/~gunnora/sacspace.htm

santiago de compostella
www.xacobeo.es/index1_ing.htm
www.crtvg.es/CamWeb/priquintana.html
http://123voyage.com/realsw/tosee/stjacqu.htm

shrines

Khwaja Moinuddin
www.campuslife.utoronto.ca/groups/sufi/CHISHTI.HTM

Ni'matallah
www.arches.uga.edu/~godlas/images/nematolah-e-vali.gif

St Paul's London
www.stpauls.co.uk/rindex.htm

stonehenge
www.keltria.org

temple

Puja: Worship in Hindu Temples
www.si.edu/asia/puja/temples.html

Shikolu Pilgrimage, Japan
www.mandala.ne.jp/echoes/jhguide.html

Teotihuacan, Mexico
http://archaeology.la.asu.edu/teo/

Wat Arun, Thailand
www.bu.ac.th/thailand/arun.html

Zatathushtra Cyber Temple
www.zarathustra.com

vatican
www.vatican.va/

sacred texts and teachings online

Sacred Texts are available in a variety of online digitised formats. While some may simply be scanned versions of printed sources, others have been built around considerable investment of time, technology and money to bring sacred texts into the 21st century. Searchable, often accompanied by notes and audio versions these texts are often supported by religious organisations, who see them as important to the development and expansion of their religions. Many of these sites are designed for use by existing believers with expertise, or for academics, which can make them heavy going for the general reader. Some are incorporated here for reasons of inclusivity, rather than because they represent 'good sites' to visit. This selection of sacred writings, revelation, inspiration, interpretation, divine texts and logos traverses diverse faith experiences. They may be available in different interpretative versions and translations, reflecting specific worldviews.

www.sacred-texts.com/
Sacred Texts

Overall rating: ★ ★ ★ ★ ★			
Classification:	Library	Readability:	★ ★ ★ ★
Updating:	Regularly	Content:	★ ★ ★ ★ ★
Navigation:	★ ★ ★ ★ ★	Speed:	★ ★ ★ ★

US

This collection of electronic religious texts, associated with diverse worldviews, was founded in 1997. The main page clearly links the reader to the principal areas of Eastern, Western, Traditional and Esoteric. Some might argue that these are not useful headings, and that the best place to start surfing texts is from the Site Map. This is linked on the top of the page. The presentation and content is very impressive, not just focusing on the 'key texts', but also on commentaries, supplements, and other writings. Sections are well resourced. A substantial amount of the content has been scanned from books and articles in the public domain. Certain texts have not been published elsewhere on the internet.

SPECIAL FEATURES

Christianity gives an indication of the site's depth, easily matched in other site areas. There is a hypertext Bible, which can be viewed in the King James version, Latin Vulgate, Greek New Testament, and Hebrew versions. Elsewhere in the Christianity section are 28 documents, ranging from a Latin mass to the Pilgrim's Progress.

Sacred Sexuality demonstrates the diversity within the site, with Tantra, the Kama Sutra, Japanese creation myths, and Ovids' love poetry available.

African contains Xhosa folklore, Bantu myths, Yoruba religious information, and a book on fetishism in west Africa. The material dates from prior to 1933 (out of print and in the public domain). Writers' attitudes of the period should be taken into account when reading, but the material is unique to the internet.

The Internet Book of Shadows is a large collection of neo-pagan texts and advice, largely preserved from postings on internet bulletin boards from the 1980s and early 1990s. As such, they have a dated format, but it is laudable that they have been preserved in this basic form.

Esoteric and Occult contains alchemy, spiritualism, Nostradamus, Rosicrucian, tarot, and other texts.

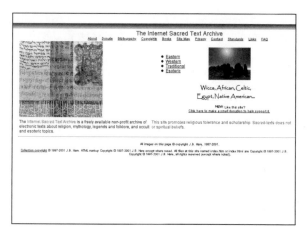

OTHER FEATURES

The Bookstore links to Amazon.com, but also contains useful advice on tracking down specific texts.

An excellent online library, drawn from different faiths, making it an excellent starting point for reading in depth about religion.

other textual sources

Aum Shinrikyo
www.aum-shinrikyo.com/english/index.htm
Teaching of AUM Supreme Truth

Bahai – Kitáb-i-Aqdas
http://metalab.unc.edu/Bahai/Texts/English/AQD/AQD-4.html

Branch Davidians – The David Koresh Manuscript: Exposition Of The Seven Seals
http://home.maine.rr.com/waco/manuscript.html

Buddhist

Access to Insight – Readings in Theravada Buddhism
www.accesstoinsight.org/index.html

Collection of Mahayana Buddhist Sutras in English
www.best.com/~mlee/

Digital Buddhist Library
http://ccbs.ntu.edu.tw/

The Electronic Bodhidharma
www.iijnet.or.jp/iriz/index_e.html

Theravada.net
http://theravada.net/

Tibetan Text Preservation
www.nyingma.org/yd/ydhome.html

Christianity

Bible Gateway
http://bible.gospelcom.net/

Book of Mormon
http://etext.virginia.edu/mormon.html

Carmelite Literature
www.ocd.or.at/lit/eng.htm

Christian Classics Ethereal Library
http://ccel.wheaton.edu/

Coptic- Digital Coptic Stuff
http://church.salib.com/

Quakers' Library
www.quaker.org.uk/index.html

Septuagint with Apocrypha: English
www.ccel.org/bible/brenton/

Shaker Manuscripts on-line
www.passtheword.org/SHAKER-MANUSCRIPTS/

Syrian Orthodox Resources
www.netadventure.com/~soc/

Falun Dafa/Falun Gong

Zhuan Falun
www.falundafa.org/

Gnosticsm

The Gnostic Society Library
www.webcom.com/~gnosis/library.html

Hare Krishna

Krishna Internet Radio Station
www.chantandbehappy.com

Sastra
www.iskcon.org/sastra/

Hinduism

Bhagavad Gita
www.iconsoftec.com/gita/

The Divya Prabandham
www.ramanuja.org/sv/prabandham/index.html

Upanishads
http://ee.memphis.edu/~sreedhar/Upanisad/frames/hinduism.html

Islam

Harf Information Technology – Qur'an
www.harf.com

Qur'an Comparative Browser
http://goon.stg.brown.edu/quran_browser/pqeasy.shtml

Jainism

Jainism Resource Centre
www.fas.harvard.edu/~pluralsm/affiliates/jainism/

Judaism

Torah – Yashanet
www.yashanet.com/library/early.htm

Rastafarianism

Sayings of Jah Rasta Fari
www.westworld.com/~jahred/rasta1.html

Shintoism

Sacred Texts – The Nihongi
www.sacred-texts.com/shi/

Sikhism

Granth (scriptures)
www.sikhs.org/

Taoism

Book of Changes (I Ching) – I-Ching on the Net
www.pacificcoast.net/~wh/index.html

Tao-te Ching – English Translations of the Tao-te Ching
www.clas.ufl.edu/users/gthursby/taoism/ttc-list.htm

Zoroastrian scriptures – Avesta
www.avesta.org/avesta.html

If you haven't found the text you are seeking, try:

Religion and Scriptures
www.wam.umd.edu/~stwright/rel/

buying books on world religions

Amazon
www.amazon.co.uk
www.amazon.com

Barnes and Noble
www.barnesandnoble.com

The Amazon resources are good places to locate information on current publications about faith and religion. Type 'religion' into the search engine to locate the appropriate pages. In the Amazon UK site, we particularly liked the list of best-selling books and CDs. The Barnes and Noble pages also produce a substantial listing of books via their search engine.

religious people

How can religious people be classified? On the internet, they can be found under a variety of banners. This introductory Who's Who of Religion includes prophets, apostles, founders, authorities, intermediaries and aspects of the divine, religious leaders, and otherwise sacred people. They have been listed according to last names (where appropriate). If they all sat around a table to discuss religion, the cutlery would soon be flying, although there are some natural alliances on this list. Some of the links point to specific pages, rather than general sites. If you are not sure who some of the individuals are on this list, why not check out their URL?

Adam
www.biblemysteries.com/library/adam/

Archbishop of Canterbury
www.cfe.anglican.org

Meher Baba
www.AvatarMeherBaba.org/

David Berg
www.thefamily.org/

Yogi Bhajan
www.yogibhajan.com

Madame Blavatsky
www.blavatsky.net/

William & Catherine Booth
www.salvationarmy.org.uk/

Louis Farrakhan
www.noi.org

St Francis
www.ofm.org/

Siddhartha Gautama (The Buddha)
www.buddhanet.net/budnetp.htm

Billy Graham
www.billygraham.org

L. Ron Hubbard
www.lronhubbard.org/

Jesus Christ
www.phoenixnewtimes.com/extra/gilstrap/jesus.html
www.newadvent.org/cathen/08374c.htm

Ruhollah Khomeini
http://irna.com/occasion/ertehal/index-e.htm

Martin Luther King
http://martinlutherking.8m.com/

David Koresh
www.sevenseals.com

Kyososama (Kanichi Otsuka)
www.shinreikyo.or.jp/html_e/jiseki_e.htm

Dalai Lama
www.dalailama.com

Martin Luther
www.iclnet.org/pub/resources/text/wittenberg/wittenberg-luther.html

Maharaji
www.maharaji.org/

St Mary
http://pharos.bu.edu/cn/pictures/Icon.StMary-1.gif

Thomas Merton
http://140.190.128.190/merton/merton.html

Sun Myung Moon
www.ettl.co.at/unification /

Moses
www.christusrex.org/www1/sistine/A-Moses.html

Muhammad
http://islam.org/radio/ch1100.htm
www.muhammad.net

Muhammad's Companions
www.umr.edu/~msaumr/reference/companions/

Elijah Muhammad
www.seventhfam.com/noilinks.htm

John Henry Newman
http://ic.net/~erasmus/raz22.htm

Osho/Rajnesshism
www.osho.com

Papacy
www.vatican.va/

Paramahansa Yogananda
www.yogananda-srf.org/

Pope Shenouda III
www.copticpope.org

Mother Theresa
www.tisv.be/mt/indmt.htm

Karma Thinley Rinpoche
www.dechen.org/

saints (christian)

The following sites contain extensive libraries of information on specific saints. Several of the sites have internal search engines.

Bollandistes
www.kbr.be/~socboll/

Cyberdesert
http://users/otenet.gr/~marinarb

Hagiography
http://orb.rhodes.edu/encyclop/religion/hagiography/hagindex.html

Internet Medieval Sourcebook: Saints' Lives
www.fordham.edu/halsall/sbook3.html

St. Pachomius Library
www.ocf.org/OrthodoxPage/reading/St.Pachomius/globalindex.html

St. Patrick's Church for All the Saints
http://users.erols.com/saintpat/ss/ss-index.htm

Patron Saints' Index
www.catholic-forum/saints/indexsnt.htm

Saints of the Orthodox Church
www.goarch.org/access/Companion_to_Orthodox_Church/Saints.html

Haille Selassie
www.blackmind.com/Phiya/throne.html

Asahara Shoko
www.aum-shinrikyo.com/english/index.htm

Gobind Singh
www.sikhs.org

Joseph Smith
www.xmission.com/~research/about/

Emanuel Swedenborg
www.newchurch.org/

St. Thomas
http://members.aol.com/manj/odox.htm

Baal Shem Tov
www.chabad.org/

Claude Vorilhon
www.rael.org/

Yahweh ben Yahweh
www.yahwehbenyahweh.com/

John Wesley
http://wesley.nnu.edu/wesley.html

Bringham Young
www.lds.org/

online authority

Do you have a question about religion? Why not consult with an 'expert'? Expertise ranges from traditionally trained religious scholars, to 'amateur authorities': individuals with a few reference books and a modem. There's plenty of choice available online, and these pages make fascinating viewing. Many sites listed under individual religious categories have FAQ (Frequently Asked Questions), or email addresses where specific questions can be sent to an online 'authority'. The following selection leads directly to diverse web pages, for the submission of questions, and/or the access to previously asked questions. There are other authorities out there in cyberspace, who have been discussed elsewhere in this book. Take care if disclosing personal information, as your enquiry may be made available for the world to see. Don't part with cash for questions.

african traditional religion

Church Of The Lukumi Babalu Aye
www.church-of-the-lukumi.org/

baha'i

Bahá'í Faith Index
www.bcca.org~cvoogt/

buddhism

Ask the Lama
www.beliefnet.com/author/author_75.html

christianity

Ask the Amish
www.800padutch.cm/askamish.html

Ask the Vicar
www.church.co.uk

Church Net UK
www.churchnet.org.uk

Opus Dei
http://cti.itc.virginia.edu/~jkh8x/soc257/nrms/dei.html

Oxford Diocese
http://oxford.anglican.org/

Watchtower Bible & Tract Society
www.watchtower.org

hinduism

Hinduism FAQ
www.hinduism.org

islam

Al-Islam
www.al-islam.org/

Ask the Imam
http://islam.org/islamicity/dialogue/a1.htm

Islam Online
www.islamonline.com

jainism

Jainism Resource Centre – FAQ
www.fas.harvard.edu/~pluralsm/affiliates/jainism/

judaism

Ask the Rabbi – Aish HaTorah
http://aish.com/

Orthodox Union
www.ou.org/

Dear Rabbi
www.jewishfamily.com

Reform Judaism
http://rj.org/

new age

Alt.Pagan
http://homepage.mac.com/paganrain/altpagfaq.html

Henge of Keltria FAQ
www.keltria.org

sikhism

Sikhism FAQ
www.sikhs.org

swami

Ask the Guru (Sri Swami Satchidananda Maharaj)
www.korrnet.org/gurutalk/

science and religion

Science and Religion introduces key issues and questions relating to interpretation of sacred texts and approaches towards the Divine. Creation theory, bio-ethics and technology have all been controversial topics addressed by various groups and individuals on the internet. A definitive list of reviews would take many pages. Whether you are a scientist, a sceptic, a believer, or simply curious, this set of thematic links will get you started. The sites below introduce many different perspectives, lively dialogues and arguments between, within and outside of religious groupings. Web addresses relate to specific pages associated with a theme.

creation

Agnostic

Agnostic Home Page
http://atheism.about.com/culture/atheism/msubmenu15.htm

Agnostic Home Page presents a sceptical perspective. This link site has material on a broad range of themes (800+ links), including science and religion. The above link locks into creationism, and presents an overview of related sites.

Christian

Creation Science
http://emporium.turnpike.net/C/cs/

Representing one evangelical approach towards the teaching of science: 'Creationism is not "against" modern science! In fact, the Biblical mandate to "subdue" the earth (Genesis 1:28) requires us to understand it, which is what science is all about. "Creation Science" is simply the practice of science with the assumption and acknowledgement that there is a creator God, versus the now standard operating assumption of naturalism (that nature is "all there is").' There is a substantial amount of interesting material on this site, which is not 'against' science, but feels that the Divine should be represented within the teaching of creation in the classroom.

Myths in Genesis
www.users.uswest.net/~rjwsr/myths/

Perhaps the opposite of Creation Science, it seeks to challenge what is perceives as 'extreme' Evangelical approaches towards the teaching of creation: 'This page does not dispute the existence of God or the possibility of the divine creation of the Universe. It goes only to the obvious myths in the first few chapters of the Book of Genesis and the attempts of the Evangelicals to force their teaching in public schools.'

Seventh Day Adventist
www.cs.unc.edu/~plaisted/ce/

'This page shows how it is possible to reconcile a literal reading of Genesis with a surprising amount of the scientific evidence. We do not mean to criticize those who support the theory of evolution, but for one who is willing to accept the possibility of supernatural intervention, we believe that a creation theory is an acceptable alternative.'

Hindu

The Puranic Accounts of Creation
www.hindumythology.com/creation.htm

Quoting from the Rigveda, this presents a Hindu perspective on creation, both of the universe and of the gods.

Islam

How Islam Views the Universal Creation
http://al-islam1.org/inquiries/4.html

Based around 'Inquiries About Islam' by Imam Mohamad Jawad Chirri, this is presented in a discussion format, and presents a Shia oriented view of creation.

Judaism

Virtual Yeshiva
www.rasheit.org/VY_LIBRARY/libminyan.html

Rabbi Rami Shapiro presents his thoughts on the subject of creation, in between his discussion on the Philosophy of Judaism. In doing so, he discusses alternative approaches within Judaism to the subject of creation.

Miscellaneous

Metaphysics, Human Experience and Nature
http://home.earthlink.net/~rlphen/index.html

Perspectives on process theological approaches towards creation, evolution, and molecular biology, which can get quite technical in terms of the science discussed.

SpiriTech Virtual Foundation
www.geocities.com/~spiritechuk/

'Spiritech Virtual Foundation is dedicated to the spiritual use and perception of cyberspace and high technology as a tool for human growth and development at all levels... A better life is possible through technology. Think like a machine, but improve your system by acting from the heart. The resources at your fingertips are nearly endless.' There, feel better now you've been at your computer for hours?

Theology and Science
http://sites.netscape.net/shaunhenson/theoscience

A series of articles and links, reflecting its author's own research interests in the field.

medicine

Buddhism

Buddhism and Medical Ethics
http://jbe.la.psu.edu/2/dkhughes.html

An academic page, discussing Buddhist approaches towards suffering, disease, compassion, and bioethics.

Christianity

Biblical Model for Medical Ethics
www.cmds.org/Ethics/1_4.htm

Presented by the Christian Medical and Dental Society, questions are raised on how the Bible can be integrated with practical medical care. Oaths are suggested for Christian Doctors and Dentists (but not for patients).

Catholic Resources for Medical Ethics
www.usc.edu/hsc/info/newman/resources/ethics.html

Declarations and guidelines on issues such as euthanasia, abortion, care for the dying, and genetic manipulation.

Islam

Islam and Medicine
http://members.muslimsites.com/skalghazal/psychology.htm

Dr. Sharif Kaf Al-Ghazal's site is very comprehensive, containing articles and materials in English and Arabic, on subjects such as psychology, sexuality, medicine, medical history, embryology, and natural medicine.

Judaism

Thirteen Principles of Jewish Medical Ethics
http://members.aol.com/Sauromalus/

Written by Harofei Yaakov Ben Ben-Tzion Halevi, this integrates advice on healing, prevention, and treatment with quotations from the Torah.

Virtual Jerusalem
www.szmc.org.il/machon/jewmed.htm

Articles on cloning, abortion, genetic engineering, and organ transplantation, linked to academic sources on Jewish Medical Ethics.

religion, gender and sexuality

Gender and sexuality issues can often be found at the roots of religion, in doctrine and sacred texts. These sites specialise in this subject, often presenting material that is unavailable elsewhere on the internet. Subjects can be controversial, and potentially contrary to traditional worldviews. In some cases, site authors are attempting to reconcile their personal orientation with their faith, and find the internet a means to dialogue with like-minded individuals.

www.hobrad.com/and.htm
And Adam Knew Eve

Overall rating: ★ ★ ★ ★		
Classification: Reference	**Readability:**	★ ★ ★
Updating: Occasionally	**Content:**	★ ★ ★ ★
Navigation:	**Speed:**	★ ★

US

This is subtitled 'A Dictionary of Sex in the Bible', and was written by Ronald L Ecker. It is serious and well-informed, rather than deliberately salacious. Navigate via the front page, which lists the key areas of the site, adjacent to an image from Hieronymus Bosch's Paradise.

SPECIAL FEATURES

A-Z lists subject matter ranging from Abraham and Sarah's marriage through to the virgin birth. References are made to other sources throughout the dictionary's entries, which are written in an accessible style. Articles are cross-referenced by hyperlinks. Expect a substantial amount of begatting and going forth and multiplying.

OTHER FEATURES

The book of the website can be purchased through these pages.

A great idea, which is well executed, and in an ideal format for mature internet consumption.

www.tantra.com/
Tantric Sex and Kama Sutra

Overall rating: ★ ★ ★ ★

Classification:	Commercial	**Readability:**	★ ★ ★ ★
Updating:	Occasionally	**Content:**	★ ★ ★ ★
Navigation:	★ ★ ★	**Speed:**	★ ★ ★

US 18

Unlike the Shiva Shakti Mandalam: Tantrik Home Page (reviewed in Hinduism, Chapter Two) this is a commercially driven site, with opportunities to buy various publications and recordings. Navigate via the right-hand side bar, if you are shopping. The site has a secure facility. Scroll down the left side bar for information. The main content of the page is summarised articles. Throughout the site, the navigation is consistent.

SPECIAL FEATURES

What is Tantra? offers seven perspectives, containing useful extracts from books on Tantric techniques, which one author describes as follows: 'Tantra teaches that lovemaking between a man and woman, when entered into with awareness, is a gateway to both sexual and spiritual ecstasy.' (Nitya Lacroix, What is Tantric Sex? www.tantra.com/mission/lacroix.html).

Kama Sutra Positions presents descriptions and illustrations from this religious text.

OTHER FEATURES

Radio Interviews offers a weekly live radio discussion forum, where Suzie Human, an 'authority on Tantra', answers questions. Requires RealPlayer.

The content may not be universally appreciated, but the western synthesis of Buddhist, Hindu, New Age, and Tantric thought in the area of sexual practices is certainly a dynamic phenomenon.

www.queerjihad.web.com/
Queer Jihad

Overall rating: ★ ★ ★			
Classification: Portal		**Readability:**	★ ★ ★
Updating: Regularly		**Content:**	★ ★ ★ ★
Navigation: ★ ★ ★ ★		**Speed:**	★ ★ ★

US

This includes a series of articles on Islam and homosexuality, and a comprehensive series of links to other pages of related interest. The site's author, Sulayman X, has been the target of vitriolic email since Queer Jihad emerged on the web.

SPECIAL FEATURES

Essays and Articles contains accounts from gay Muslims relating to their lifestyle and identity, together with related opinion pieces and stories.

Links introduces a broad range of related websites and discussion groups, associated with diverse interests and orientations.

There is plenty of general interest information relating to reconciling sexual and religious-cultural identity.

OTHER SITES OF INTEREST

Culture and Religion
www.afao.org.au/gayguys/culture.html

'The clearest things we can say about culture, religion and men who are attracted to other men are, firstly, that same sex desire appears in almost all cultures throughout history. Secondly, attitudes toward same sex desire, and laws about it, differ between and within cultures and religions.' This Australian site presents a brief issue of identity and religious issues, and a series of links to various local religious organisations with gay and lesbian agendas.

CyberSangha – Tantric Buddhism and Sexuality
www.worldtrans.org/CyberSangha/mckinw95.htm

CyberSangha features a conversation between two 'feminists', discussing sexuality and related issues from Buddhist perspectives.

Homosexuality and Theravada Buddhism
www.zip.com.au/~lyallg/homo.htm

Discusses the ethical and religious dimensions of homosexuality, and reaches the following conclusion: 'Certainly the loathing, fear and hatred that the western homosexual has so often had to endure is absent and this is due, to a very large degree, to Buddhism's humane and tolerant influence.'

Homosexuality and the Bible
http://christianity.about.com/culture/christianity/library/weekly/aa091597.htm

'Christians of several denominations are today involved in a painful and difficult debate over the degree to which lesbian and homosexual persons should be welcomed to serve as ministers or in other capacities as leaders of churches.' This site presents opposing papers on the issue, and invites readers to respond.

Muslim Women's League – An Islamic Perspective on Sexuality
www.islamzine.com/women/xuality.html

This is very much an overview, presenting interpretations and perspectives on issues such as marriage, contraception, abortion, homosexuality, and sex education. It draws upon the Qur'an and other Islamic source material.

Ontario Centre of Religious Tolerance
www.religioustolerance.org/homosexu.htm

A series of essays on bisexuality and homosexuality, including sermons and pages on subjects such as Conflicts with Christianity over Homosexuality, Policies of Religious Groups Towards Gays, Lesbians and Homosexuality, Homophobia, and 'Healing' of Gays and Lesbians.

Ramakrishna
www.sonic.net/~danslist/GayLove/GayLove.htm

A web page written by a gay Tantric monk, discussing his 'recovery' from the ravages of AIDS.

SageWoman
www.sagewoman.com/

Drawing from the magazine Sage Woman, there's an entertaining selection of articles and links on these pages. They operate under the slogan 'Celebrating the goddess in every woman', and link into several new age-oriented publications.

SisterSite
www.geocities.com/Wellesley/1114/

This is a Catholic resource seeking 'to serve as a clearing house for information on women's religious congregations, the history of religious life, and the contemporary concerns of women in church and society'. It contains a broad range of material, going outside of Catholicism, including links to various religious communities, information on academic sources, and resources on women's studies, including theology and spirituality.

World Congress of Gay, Lesbian, and Bisexual Jewish Organizations
www.wcgljo.org/index.html

Offers free prayer books, news, a journal, and regular conferences and meetings.

sacred food

There are many links to food sections contained on pages listed elsewhere in this book. Here are a few selected sites, which focus directly on food in relation to religion or religious-cultural identities.

www.superluminal.com/cookbook/index_flat_essays.html
Serving the Guest: a Sufi Cookbook and Art Gallery

Overall rating: ★ ★ ★ ★ ★			
Classification: Information		**Readability:**	★ ★ ★ ★ ★
Updating: Regularly		**Contents:**	★ ★ ★ ★ ★
Navigation: ★ ★ ★ ★ ★		**Speed:**	★ ★ ★ ★
US			

Author Kathleen Seidel has made an outstanding application of the internet as an information resource, with good use of graphics and much fascinating content. A proportion of the site is translated and edited from Arabic, Persian, Turkish and other sources. The entire site is worth browsing, but for our purposes the cookbook section is highlighted (the URL listed takes you to the no-frames version). Navigate via the front page to main site zones.

SPECIAL FEATURES

Recipes is divided into Bread, Soup, Small Helpings, Substantial Dishes, Grain Dishes, Pastries, Halvah, Puddings, and Beverages. There are over 200 links here. Each contains a link to a detailed recipe and cooking instructions, together with an illustration and appropriate quotation. Dishes are drawn from throughout the Muslim world. Yakhni and Bakmi Goreng recipes are recommended.

Serving the Guest gives guidance relating to food and Sufism, including advice on Manners, Grace, Food and Festivals, Teachers and Traditions, Miracles and Parables, and Tales of Hospitality and Celebration. Pages contain illustrations, and source details (check Bibliography from the main page for full details). Coffee: the Wine of Islam and You Cannot Feed a Dervish were particularly enjoyable.

OTHER FEATURES

The Gallery contains a diverse selection of resources, such as calligraphy and Syrian art.

Hours of interesting browsing are available on this site, making it invaluable for anyone with an interest in religion and food.

www.jewish-food.org/
Classic Jewish Recipe Archive

Overall rating: ★ ★ ★ ★			
Classification: Recipes		**Readability:**	★ ★ ★ ★
Updating: Regularly		**Contents:**	★ ★ ★ ★
Navigation: ★ ★ ★ ★		**Speed:**	★ ★ ★ ★ ★

UK

This is a substantial database of Jewish recipes from all over the world, regularly updated, and linked to the Kosher Recipes Webring.

SPECIAL FEATURES

Search the Recipe Archive is useful if you are seeking the recipe to a particular dish. We tested 'falafel', which came up with 55 matches (including sauces, and advice on what to serve it with).

Recipes by Category divides the archive into Classics, Holidays, Latest Dishes, Deserts, International, Goodies and Passover.

The international flavour of the site and its search engine combine to make a really useful set of pages.

http://members.home.net/stoma/
Middle East Cookbook

Overall rating: ★ ★ ★ ★			
Classification: Cookbook		**Readability:**	★ ★ ★ ★
Updating: Regularly		**Contents:**	★ ★ ★ ★
Navigation: ★ ★ ★		**Speed:**	★ ★ ★

US

There are many excellent Middle Eastern cookbooks available in cyberspace, of which this is a good example. Sabria Farid Toma is an Iraqi-born grandmother, now resident in California, who spent years compiling recipes to preserve her cooking tradition for future generations. Rather than print the results, she decided to place the book onto the internet. The front page divides the site into Ingredients, Recipes, Marketplace and Author zones. The left-hand side bar lists recent additions to the site.

SPECIAL FEATURES

Recipes is divided into Entrees, Soups, Salads and Appetizers, and Desserts. The page contains some great recipes, with English names and their Arabic equivalent. The page is searchable, and the site is also linked to Egyptian and Moroccan sections.

Marketplace offers the ingredients of the recipes, which can be shipped anywhere in the world. There is a secure shopping cart facility. Recipes and suggestions are contained in relation to the ingredients.

The Middle East Cookbook is a superb hyperlinked resource to diverse foods, reflecting the religions and cultures of the region.

http://schwartz.enviroweb.org/

The Schwartz Collection on Judaism, Vegetarianism, and Animal Rights

Overall rating: ★ ★ ★ ★			
Classification:	Information	Readability:	★ ★
Updating:	Regularly	Contents:	★ ★
Navigation:	★ ★ ★ ★	Speed:	★ ★ ★ ★ ★

UK US

This is a fascinating series of articles by Richard Schwartz, low on graphics and high in text. Navigate via the front page, which lists over 100 pages relating to Judaism and vegetarianism. Key areas of the site are Judaism and Animal Issues, Health and Nutrition Issues, and Vegetarianism Activism.

SPECIAL FEATURES

Jewish Festivals and Vegetarianism is particularly interesting, given the importance of the concept of sacrifice within Judaism's history. All festivals are discussed, utilising Torah quotes and Rabbinic commentaries.

The broad range of discussions contained on this site is very useful, although some readers might have liked illustrations or graphics to augment the site.

www.kosher.org.uk/

London Beth Din Kashrut Division

Overall rating: ★ ★ ★			
Classification:	Information	Readability:	★ ★ ★
Updating:	Regularly	Contents:	★ ★
Navigation:	★ ★ ★ ★	Speed:	★ ★ ★ ★

UK

The word kosher has entered the English language. Promoted as the leading authority on Jewish Dietary laws in the United Kingdom, this site operates under the aegis of The Court of the Chief Rabbi of the United Hebrew Congregations of the Commonwealth. The site is easy to navigate via the side bar.

SPECIAL FEATURES

Kosher Updates advises on which products are kosher, or have changed status. This is a substantial list, charting the transition of status of a variety of foods (notably sweets).

Kosher Establishments lists approved bakers, caterers, delis, fish shops, food manufacturers, hotels, and restaurants. A hyperlinked version would have been useful.

OTHER FEATURES

Kosher Certification discusses the requirements of a Beth Din approved kosher *parve* status. There is an emailing list, to receive official kosher updates.

This site is a useful introduction to the concept of kosher food.

http://perso.wanadoo.fr/cyril.pagniez/Trappist.htm
Trappist Beer

Overall rating: ★ ★ ★			
Classification:	Information	Readability:	★ ★ ★
Updating:	Regularly	Contents:	★ ★ ★
Navigation:	★ ★	Speed:	★ ★ ★

FRA

Trappist beers are brewed by, or supervised by, members of the Trappist branch of the Cistercians. There is controversy as to whether the term 'Trappist' can refer to a technique of beer production, even if an Abbey does not produce that beer. This site focuses on Belgian Trappist beers produced by Abbeys. The site can be difficult to navigate, but main content can be found on the front page.

SPECIAL FEATURES

Index introduces the main Abbey-based breweries, describing their historical origins and linking to related sites of interest.

Labels (on the entry page) is illustrated by GIFs of labels from the main breweries, together with glasses and other memorabilia. There are also illustrations of 'fake' Trappist products.

This intoxicating aspect of monastic life is well represented on this enthusiast's site.

www.veg.faithweb.com/
Christian Vegetarian Association

Overall rating: ★ ★ ★			
Classification:	Information	Readability:	★ ★
Updating:	Regular	Contents:	★ ★ ★
Navigation:	★ ★ ★	Speed:	★ ★ ★ ★

UK US

The Ecumenical Christian Vegetarian Association's agenda is centred on the notion of 'witnessing to the compassion, love and peace of Christ by adopting and advocating a vegetarian diet'. They offer a monthly e-newsletter, articles and FAQs. Navigate by the side bar, which lists all site content. The banner advertising may distract some readers, especially as it was promoting gambling on a recent visit.

SPECIAL FEATURES

Questions and Answers about Christianity and Vegetarianism lists 24 hyperlinked questions, with some interesting themes, including Is vegetarianism biblical? and Didn't Jesus eat meat?

What would Jesus Eat Today? This article examines the ethical issues of food production and consumption in relation to Scripture.

OTHER FEATURES

The site offers membership, and a comprehensive annotated series of related links.

Christian Vegetarian Association have produced an interesting and easy-to-digest introduction to Christian vegetarianism.

www.almadina.co.uk/index1.html
Muslim Food Guide

Overall rating: ★ ★			
Classification:	Information	Readability:	★ ★ ★
Updating:	Regularly	Contents:	★ ★
Navigation:	★ ★ ★	Speed:	★ ★ ★ ★

UK

Muslim Food Guide discusses the ritualistic aspects of food in Islam, and promotes its related publication. The side bar lists the key areas of the site.

SPECIAL FEATURES

Articles and Fatwa provide religious opinions on specific aspects of food production and diet, such as GM Food and Takeaway Food, whilst also producing a useful glossary of terms.

Product Updates lists the latest foods deemed halal (permitted) or haram (forbidden). Search the site via a drop-down menu.

More information on the religious background to halal food production would have enhanced these pages.

OTHER SITES OF INTEREST

About.com Kosher Wines – What are they?
http://wine.about.com/food/wine/library/encyc/bl_kosher.htm

This page explains how kosher wine is closely associated with Jewish ritual. This section from About.com lists a number of producers of Kosher wine, and links to wine tasting notes and suppliers.

Biospirituality
www.vegsource.com/biospirituality/main.html

Biospirituality is a pro-vegetarian page, with a religious emphasis, offering discussion on the ethics of vegetarianism.

Buddhist Resources on Vegetarianism and Animal Welfare
http://online.sfsu.edu/~rone/Buddhism/Buddhist%20Vegetarian.htm

This page links into essential web resources on Buddhism and vegetarianism, including external links and primary texts.

Pakistani Hindu Patrika
www.geocities.com/Athens/Delphi/7295/vegetarianism.html

This is an essay on the religious significance of vegetarianism in Hinduism, and the ethics of mass food production.

Vegetarianism and Religion
www.blue-harvest.com/vegetarianism/religion.html

This contains one-page summaries relating to approaches to vegetarianism in Judaism, Hinduism and Christianity.

sacred sounds and music radio

There are thousands of stations with 'spiritual' content. Some of these are real broadcasters who also use conventional transmitters. Others are special internet stations, or simply individuals wanting to expose a particular form of music. There is a substantial amount of music that doesn't always make it to conventional radio stations. Stations require an MP3 player/RealPlayer. We have chosen music sources below which appealed to us for various reasons, but you will probably want to set up a play list to match personal musical tastes. You can do that too! Here are two methods:

www.live365.com
Live365

Overall rating: ★ ★ ★ ★ ★			
Classification:	Portal	**Readability:**	★★★★
Updating:	Regularly	**Contents:**	★★★★★
Navigation:	★★★★★	**Speed:**	★★★★

US

The front page's magazine format highlights various zones of this site, which has links to 27,943 'stations'. These range from professional broadcasters to people creating their own stations, via the software available through this site. The front page offers free membership of the site, which is useful if you want to preset your own stations, and go to them automatically every time you visit the site. The form requires you to provide email and personal details. Live365 uses a variety of listening software: RealPlayer, Windows Media Player, Winamp, Sonique, and MusicMatch are all supported. They also offer their own Player365. Details on set up can be found through the Listening Tutorial link on the front page, which is worth looking at to ensure that your computer is appropriately configured for online listening. The site is fully searchable, if you are seeking a particular genre.

SPECIAL FEATURES

Religious stations can be accessed from the front page, via the drop-down menu on the top bar. Each station has a brief description, a guide to its popularity (through the key on the right hand side of the page), modem speed information, and the broadcaster's URL. It is an eclectic mix of 600-plus wannabe DJs, preachers, music fans, and professional broadcasters from across the world. Clicking on the link activates your player. There are no guarantees of recording quality on the stations, but there is much to enjoy and, in some cases, ponder on.

Christian is accessible from the drop-down menu, and contains an interesting mix of stations, from orthodox liturgy to Christian ska, with links to talk stations and ministries across the world.

Broadcast (via About Us) enables you to set up your own radio station, if you haven't found what you are looking for in cyberspace, or simply want to proclaim your own message. All the software and tools are there. All you need is music talent, as there are some important copyright issues to consider (details on site).

OTHER FEATURES

The **World Music** section also has 'spiritual' content. The site also hosts a secure shopping facility, and provides newsletters for updates on stations and technology.

More eclectic and interactive than Real's site, there are some real gems and unusual spiritual offerings to be found throughout this site.

http://realguide.real.com/tuner/
RealPlayer – Radio Tuner

Overall rating: ★ ★ ★ ★			
Classification:	Portal	**Readability:**	★ ★ ★ ★
Updating:	Regularly	**Contents:**	★ ★ ★ ★ ★
Navigation:	★ ★ ★ ★ ★	**Speed:**	★ ★ ★
US			

RealPlayer is an essential piece of software, if you want to listen to broadcasts, audio files or view certain video material on the internet. Whilst Real is a commercial company, it does give out versions of its products for free, profiting from advertising and the possibility of customers wishing to upgrade to a superior version of the Player. Rather than download it from the internet (which can be a lengthy process), if you don't have a Player, the latest versions can usually be found on the CDs given away by computer magazines. Installation is straightforward. Once you have the Player, go online to http://realguide. real.com/tuner/. The left-hand side bar contains the main genres covered by the Player.

SPECIAL FEATURES

Spiritual is a good place to start listening to religious music on the internet. 127 stations were listed when we visited. Click on the station of your choice, and receive streaming audio. There is a hyperlink to the entire list at the bottom of the page. Each station is usually linked to a homepage, for more information about artists played, presenters and interactive opportunities. Some of the stations discussed below were located using RealPlayer. If you find something you like, click on the plus (+) sign on the listing, and add the station to your personal presets for easy access on the next visit. Make the My Stations hyperlink your homepage, and you can enjoy music immediately you log onto the web.

OTHER FEATURES

World Music contains related stations, some with multicultural outlooks, including blends of Celtic Music, Reggae, Gospel, and Soul.

A great place for free, spiritually uplifting music in various genres from around the world.

OTHER SITES OF INTEREST

A Topic of Dispute in Islam: Music
www.wakeup.org/anadolu/05/4/mustafa_sabri_en.html

A 1910 article by Ottoman scholar Mustafa Sabri, detailing one Muslim perspective on the pros and cons of music, illustrating the argument with extracts from the Qur'an.

Abbey of Solesmes
www.solesmes.com/anglais/ang_solesmes.html

One of the homes of Gregorian Chant, the Abbey produces some sublime recordings, which can be sampled on these pages. This link takes you to an explanation of liturgy, and excellent recordings of the Gloria. The left-hand side bar will direct you to other areas of interest. Requires RealPlayer.

African Music
www.africaonline.com/AfricaOnline/covermusic.html

The content changes regularly on this site, which acts as a guide to music from across Africa. A substantial proportion is related to festivals, spirituality and religious events. The site is divided into regions, each listing nations and discussing their music histories. There are selected tracks available on each page, requiring RealPlayer.

Al Green
www.algreen.com/

Known for his soul music, such as Let's Stay Together and Take Me to the River, this is Rev Al Green's official website. Go to the bookstore for samples of his current music.

Alan Godlas: Islamic Art, Architecture and Music Around the World
www.arches.uga.edu/~godlas/IslArt.html#Music.

A concise overview of different musical forms associated (by some) with Islam, including RealPlayer samples to demonstrate the diversity and complexity of these forms.

Ancient Heritage
www.ancient-heritage-magazine.com/

Pagan music radio, produced by an American magazine. Browse their articles and listen at the same time, for the full effect. Player365 or RealPlayer required.

Arabic Christian Directory
http://lost2found.tripod.com/music.html#Topic4

This is a listing of Arabic Christian music, with contributions of psalms, hymns and other recording from diverse churches, available via MP3 and RealPlayer.

Arutz Sheva
www.israelnationalnews.com/english/radio/Fradio.htm

Arutz Sheva is based in Israel, and broadcasts from a ship outside of territorial waters. The website contains a substantial music section, including a jukebox with Hassidic Hits, and live broadcasts in Hebrew, Russian, French and English. The news service is updated daily, and presents a strong pro-Israel perspective, with what it describes as 'politically conservative programming with a traditional Jewish-Zionist orientation'.

Bangla Islam Media
www.banglaislamicmedia.com

This is a real find of Bengali spiritual music, which can be heard using RealPlayer. The main page is in Bengali and English. Recordings are hyperlinked by small icons, on the left and right-hand sides of the page. Ten sections are listed, with music, poetry, children's songs and Qur'anic commentaries. The top left-hand icon takes you to Hamd, a great recording of ten tracks of music.

Belief Net
www.beliefnet.com/index/index_503.html

Part of an interesting resource focusing on world religions, the above pages are regularly updated with information about world music with a spiritual edge. This includes sample tracks, available through RealPlayer: when we visited, rapper DMX could be heard at prayer, alongside Palestinian group El Funoun's wedding music, hardcore Christian rockers POD, and songs for the pagan family. If you like what you hear, then you can buy the CD online. This general page contains links to significant areas of world music associated with faith, and their review of the Best Spiritually Uplifting music of 2000 included Johnny Cash, Aaron Neville, U2, and Westminster Cathedral Choir.

Black Gospel Network
www.oneplace.com/live_radio/bgn/bgn.asp

There are hundreds of spiritually oriented stations available on the internet. Black Gospel Network plays some classic and contemporary gospel music. The feed is good quality, and the advertising is unobtrusive. Requires RealPlayer.

Buddha Net
www.buddhanet.net/bn_audio.htm

Download Buddhist Chanting via RealPlayer. Five files were available when we visited the site, with more promised. File sizes are given, and you can buy the CD of the website.

Buddhist Lectures and Chants
www.campuslife.utoronto.ca/groups/buddhist/lectures/

An introductory selection of ritualistic chants from diverse Buddhist backgrounds, together with contemporary Buddhist music, and some explanatory lectures.

Catholic Jukebox
www.catholicjukebox.com/mor

The blend of music on the Jukebox will keep you 'entertained' for hours. We liked The Apologist, for example, who is a rapper/missionary who has played Rome. If that prospect does not appeal, there is a streaming radio station of Catholic hits. Player365 or RealPlayer required.

CCMusic
www.ccmusic.org/

Contains the Christian Music Directory, and the related Christian Artists' List, A-Z resources focusing on contemporary American Christian Music.

Christian Pirate Radio
www.christianpirateradio.com/

Christian Pirate Radio is available in two flavours, 'rock' and 'xtreme'. You can listen to either via this main page. There are also details of the music on offer, a secure shopping cart if you want to buy some of the tracks, and daily 'devotional' content. Requires either RealPlayer, Player365, Windows Media Player, or choose their Web Radio option (no plug-in or player required).

Diamond Way Buddhism: Tibetan Music
www.diamondway-buddhism.org/terms/music.htm

A brief overview of Tibetan music, accompanied by examples of chants and instrumentation. 'The Lamas say "Religion is sound". The recitation of mantras, chanting and the playing of instrumental music are fundamental in their worship.'

Devotional Music
www.balaji.net/html/a14music.html

Indices of RealAudio and MP3 devotional music downloads, brought to you by Hong Kong-based devotees of Lord Venkateswara.

Extreme Christian Music
www.christianhxc.cjb.net/

Hardcore and death metal, from bands such as Acoustic Torment, Tortured Conscience and Mortification. We can't vouch for the quality of the music, but the site does have curiosity value. Player365, RealPlayer, MP3 or cotton wool required.

Gurbani Kirtan – Live
www.gurbani.org/kirtan.htm

Listen to Shabad Gurbani, Sikh Holy Scripture. There is a selection of more than 30 titles, based on the writings of Sri Guru Granth Sahib, and available in RealPlayer format.

Jammin Reggae Virtual Radio
www.niceup.com/

Given that reggae has been integral to the spiritual development of the Rastafarian religion, this resource is a great entry point to hear a broad range of music (some of which is faith oriented). The main zones are hyperlinked at the top of the page, including Sounds, Tours and Win Stuff. Musical genres are listed on the left-hand side bar. The front page is loaded with links to other areas of the site, and navigation can be slightly confusing at times. MP3 downloads are available, together with links to online music stores and other online reggae radio stations. Jammin Reggae Virtual Radio allows you to sample different musical styles from the site's own station. Reggae Archives clarifies the site. From here, navigate to Roots for a selection of links to 'conscious' sounds. Bob Marley and Reggae History are also good jump pages. Patois is a dictionary of terminology. Requires RealPlayer.

Jewish Music WebCenter
www.jmwc.org/index.html

Jewish Music WebCenter is an academic site, clearly listing all aspects of Jewish music, from websites to information about specific musicians.

Joyful Noise
www.lisco.com/leo/joyful/catholic.html

A resource list of Catholic music, primarily with a contemporary edge, including performers, music companies, and links.

Mythological Origins of Sangeet
http://chandrakantha.com/articles/indian_music/

'Sangeet is a combination of three artforms: vocal music, instrumental music and dance'. This site explains all about North Indian music, including its historical and technical development. Samples of various forms of Indian music, which has its roots in Hindu beliefs, are provided.

Pakistani Music Channel: Nusrat Fateh Ali Khan
www.muziq.net/artists/nfak/songs.shtml
www.pakistanimusic.com/music/qawwali/
http://members.fortunecity.com/nfak4all

Nusrat Fateh Ali Khan (1948-97), Pakistan's premier singer and exponent of devotional music (qawwali), had a popularity which transcended his religious and cultural background. Khan has a number of websites devoted to his uplifting Sufi mystical music. Pakistani Music Channel has more than 100 tracks for download using RealPlayer or MP3. Qawwali has a market way beyond its traditional Muslim audience in the Indian subcontinent.

ProudToBeSikh
www.proudtobesikh.com/

A selection of Sikh oriented jukeboxes and radio stations, including content for children, and Punjabi music. Player365 or RealPlayer required.

Radiou
http://radiou.com/

Their diverse playlist includes a trance, techno and Christian synthesis. Player365 required.

Sacred Music and Liturgy Resources
www.chesco.com/~cjcigas/

'This site is all about sharing information on sacred music and other liturgy resources that may be useful to liturgists, music directors, choir directors and musicians of all denominations'. Catholic centred, but with links to other branches of Christianity.

Siteworthy
www.siteworthy.com/

Siteworthy describes its output as 'the hottest in Christian rock/hard rock/metal/rapcore'. Player365 or RealPlayer required.

Sufi Music
http://yangtze.cs.uiuc.edu/~jamali/sindh/res/ram-music.html

A wide range of Islamic devotional music is available here, from Sindhi cultural contexts. Sample tracks using a RealPlayer, and buy via Amazon.com.

The Music Magazine
www.themusicmagazine.com/

Reviews of the latest music from the Indian subcontinent, including religious music, but unfortunately no sound files. Useful as a guide of what to buy (if you can track it down).

Torah Portions
http://bible.ort.org/bible/index/inx_tora.htm

A resource for those seeking to approach and pronounce the Torah: 'Each page shows two versions of the Hebrew text: a notated version with vowels, punctuation and musical notation; and an unnotated one, as it appears in the Torah scroll. An English translation and transliteration are also included, and audio files demonstrate the chanting of every verse.'

Vaanoli – Hindu Devotional Music
www.vaanoli.com/

This devotional channel contains over fourteen hours of religious music. They also take requests. Elsewhere, there's a rich source of Hindi music. Vaanoli has a variety of listening options, including Player365, RealPlayer 7, Winamp, Sonique and MP3.

Zemerl
www.princeton.edu/zemerl/

Drawing from a variety of music traditions, this is an interactive database of 500-plus songs, including Hassidic, Israeli and Yiddish music. They are classified in Family, Holiday, and Miscellaneous sections. Tracks come with translations, lyrics and RealPlayer sound files. Surfers are invited to send in their own songs, to augment the database.

humour

Humour and religion may seem at times to be an unlikely mixture, but there is plenty of amusing material to be found about faith, even on purportedly serious websites. Many religious traditions also pay attention to the humorous. After all, sermons and homilies often contain a punch line, designed to make a speech memorable or otherwise interesting. The following selection of websites contains a range of material. Some are parody sites with a serious underlying theme; others are 'serious' religious sites introducing the subject of humour to their discourse. Whether you find them funny or not (it's all a matter of taste), they add to the rich discourse about faith available in cyberspace, and as such surfers interested in religious themes should be made aware of them.

www.exit109.com/~mcluff/bible.shtml
Biblical Indecency for the Theologically Correct

Overall rating: ★ ★ ★			
Classification:	Humour	**Readability:**	★ ★ ★
Updating:	Regularly	**Contents:**	★ ★
Navigation:	★ ★ ★	**Speed:**	★ ★

(INT)

Biblical Indecency for the Theologically Correct raises some significant issues relating to censorship, drawing upon quotations from the Bible to state its case: '"There she lusted after her lovers, whose genitals were like those of donkeys and whose emission was like that of horses. So you longed for the lewdness of your youth, when in Egypt your bosom was caressed and your young breasts fondled." Ezekiel 23:20-21 New International Version. So many of the Theologically Correct crowd worry about their youths leering

at skinful computer screens...yet remain unaware of the "filth" within their beloved Bible'. As if to prove their point, there is an exhaustive list of further quotes, hyperlinked to versions of the Bible. Navigate the site via the side bar, or scroll down the page to read selected quotations.

SPECIAL FEATURES

Reactions to Biblical Indecency indicate a broad response to the site. From the mail they have received, clearly a number of people are angry about this site. Those of a sensitive disposition might prefer not to read Weird Responses or Hellfire and Brimstone Replies, although Thoughtful Replies contains some interesting responses relating to freedom of speech.

The thoughtful responses to biblical quotations contained on this site, from people of diverse backgrounds, make this site a stimulating one.

http://chelsea.ios.com/~hkarlin1/welcome.html			
First Presleyterian Church			
Overall rating: ★ ★ ★			
Classification: Information		**Readability:**	★ ★ ★
Updating: Occasionally		**Contents:**	★ ★ ★
Navigation: ★ ★		**Speed:**	★ ★ ★
US			

Assuming that they're not being serious here (maybe we just have a Suspicious Mind), this 'Church' has created icons, a 'testament', rumours about an anti-Elvis, and, most importantly of all, opportunities to buy the T-shirt of the church. Scroll down the page to view the icons associated with key features, or join the Church.

SPECIAL FEATURES

The Contract with Elvis describes a campaign to include Presley on the Mount Rushmore monument, and even provides an artistic impression of the revised sculpture. There's a complete list of US Senators to email, if you haven't got anything better to do.

Photo Page indicates that the Presleytarians have a good time preaching the gospel according to Elvis.

Not exactly rocking, but a bizarre manifestation of Presley in Cyberspace.

www.jesusoftheweek.com/index.html			
Jesus of the Week			
Overall rating: ★ ★ ★			
Classification: Humour		**Readability:**	★ ★
Updating: Weekly		**Contents:**	★ ★ ★ ★
Navigation: ★ ★ ★ ★		**Speed:**	★ ★ ★ ★
US			

Jesus of the Week actually introduces serious issues relating to the depiction of Jesus Christ, and the commercialisation of his image.

SPECIAL FEATURES

Jesus of the Week can be navigated via the drop-down menu at the top of the page. There are over 150 Jesus images on the site. Some of the images are 'serious', taken from religious art or books. Others are spoofs, created by liberal application of desktop publishing software. Sometimes it is difficult to determine the difference between the serious and the parody. We were particularly taken with Jesus Action Figure and Jesus Loves Denver.

An original and thought-provoking site, illustrating the range of human imagination of the divine. It's also very funny.

http://home.ptd.net/~krill/sopm/sters.html			
Sisters of Perpetual Misery			
Overall rating: ★ ★ ★			
Classification: Humour		**Readability:**	★ ★ ★
Updating: Occasionally		**Contents:**	★ ★ ★
Navigation: ★ ★		**Speed:**	★ ★
US			

Sisters of Perpetual Misery operates under the motto 'To Serve God and Man Miserably'. Navigate their site via the right-hand sidebar, which includes Suffering Requests, Ministries, and St. Paxamander's Online Gift Shop.

SPECIAL FEATURES

Net Nun is the Sisters' very own software: 'Net Nun automatically launches when you start up your web browser and sits quietly between the browser and your internet connection vigilantly comparing its immense knowledge base of heathen terms, concepts, dogmas and doctrines to the data stream flowing into your computer. If so much as one apostate byte attempts to get to your screen Net Nun springs into action performing a virtual exorcism to prevent your young impressionable child from viewing non-Catholic rubbish'.

Some people might wish that Net Nun really worked! Also see Net Moses (below).

OTHER HUMOUROUS SITES

Adult Christianity
www.jesus21.com

'Defending the rights of the un-born again'. There's some amusing material here. Check out the Christian Women Wrestlers. The site also has a critical and serious edge, with a broad resource base of materials about Christianity and Christians, presented by those who are sceptical or have left churches. This includes up-to-date news stories with a religious theme.

Ask Sister Rosetta
www.rossetta.com/

Dedicated to Jennifer Lopez, 'Latina goddess', this site is a lot of fun. It contains a spoof advice page, providing answers to questions using biblical quotations and concepts. Judging by the Sepulchre's archive of old questions, there seems to be an unhealthy emphasis on biblically approved undergarments, and nun's clothing (witness Areala, the Warrior Nun).

Balaam's Ass Speaks
www.balaams-ass.com/

A strong satirical edge, not for the easily offended, on a site that focuses on Christianity, but has diversified into comments on Islam. Arguments are linked to 'authentic' religious sites, and opportunities to purchase various source materials. Try and work out whether any of this is for real (especially the information about piano tuning).

Biography of the Final Messenger
www.prophetmuhammed.org/docs/character31.html

Drawing upon examples from the sayings and biography of Muhammad, this page is part of a most extensive site representing the Prophet's characteristics, and suggests that, amongst his other qualities, he had a sense of humour.

Craggy Island Examiner
www.geocities.com/Paris/2694/craggy.html

This is an unofficial site relating to the Craggy Island Parish. Read about the activities of Father Ted, Father Jack and Father Dougal. The Examiner contains details on the geography of the island, episodes, and ecumenical matters.

First Church of Jesus Christ, Elvis
http://jubal.westnet.com/hyperdiscordia/sacred_heart_elvis.html

'For unto you is born this day in the city of Memphis a Presley, which is Elvis the King'. Pictures of 'the King', drawing upon Christian iconography, illustrate this site, which is based on a book. Well, I suppose it depends on your sense of humour. The site also links into other Elvis/'religious' pages.

Goodness Gracious Me
www.comedyzone.beeb.com/ggm/ggm_home.html

The website of the BBC TV and radio series, which had as one focus the experiences of people of Indian subcontinent ancestry living in the UK. Mullahs, priests, 'the Guru', and others of a religious persuasion were all considered fair targets.

Jesus Is Lord Escort Ministries
http://tammysplace.home.mindspring.com/

Operating under the banner 'Have Bible Will Travel', this purports to be an escort agency run by 'Miss Jessup' offering 'classy and discreet personal services for the discriminating pastor'. Click on the naked lady to enter the site. You have been warned...

Jewish Humor Site
www.jewishpath.org/reststop.html

A page on 'clean' Jewish humour, featuring the (inevitable) lawyer, doctor and mother-in-law jokes.

Jokin' and Degradin'
http://users.ev1.net/~doogmeister/dcs/posts/funindex.html

This reflects the content of the alt.religion.scientology listing, providing humour and satire relating to L. Ron Hubbard and Scientology. Some of the material would seem to have been shut down by Scientology law suits. The site appears somewhat dated.

Lighter Side of Buddhism
www.serve.com/cmtan/buddhism/Lighter/index.html

The Buddha is said to have had a sense of humour, although whether he would have found this page funny is another matter. This is essentially a link page to various humorous pages on Buddhism, with titles such as 'Buddhism Viruses are lurking on the web' and the 'Zen Diving Association'. How we laughed.

Mormon Zone
www.mormonzone.com/index.htm

Jokes of the following ilk: 'What did Ammon say to King Lamoni after he tended the sheep?' There over 150 others like this on this site. It's the way you tell them.

Net Moses
www.fadetoblack.com/netmoses.html

A 'net filtering system' for Christian fundamentalists, blocking out terms such as 'sex, promiscuity, idols, alcohol, tobacco, non Anglo-Saxon religions, rock music, cross dressing, joking, chanukah, flirting, laughing, dancing, having fun'. That probably only leaves five percent of the net to browse...

Suite 101 – Buddhist Humor
http://209.52.189.2/article.cfm/buddhism/16275

An article about Buddhist humour, illustrated by jokes and links to other sites. The punch lines often incorporate enlightenment.

That Old Time Religion
www.lehigh.edu/~inwht/Whispering-Trees/song:otr.html

That Old Time Religion provides lyrics to a spoof series of 'religious songs', not for the serious or perhaps the musically inclined, but amusing in their diversity and lyrical content (occasionally!).

The Jesus Dance
www.jesusdance.com/

Animated GIFs of Jesus shake, rattle and roll. Not for the easily offended Christian, or for those with limited hard drive space ...

The Lawful and the Prohibited in Islam
www.qaradawi.net/english/books/The-lawful&The-Prohibited-In-Islam/Chap4/chap4s3.htm

When is it appropriate to tell jokes in Islam? This perspective, from the scholar Yusuf Qaradawi, discusses the basic human need of humans to 'relax, and to enjoy themselves'.

The Old Testament Text Adventure
www.princeton.edu/~ahutgoff/otadventure.html

A piece of Java role playing, where you work your way through various Old Testament scenarios, and achieve a 'score' at the end: 'Welcome to the world. You, sir, are in luck, for the God of this universe has deigned you one of his chosen people. With you and your descendants he has made a covenant, an eternal promise that you will benefit from his benevolence as long as you obey the law and follow the path of the righteous. You have no boils. You have ten children. You have 100 goats. You have pottage'. Oh yes, and you can also email God.

Yeshua Connection
www.torahbytes.org/sechel/smiles.htm

Did you hear the one about the rabbi and the astronaut? You will here, complete with references to Shul and tefellin. Note: some of the punchlines are in Hebrew.

further surfing

If you still haven't found what you were looking for, then one of these entry points should be useful. They are all substantial general listings, providing links to resources. Try to narrow down the parameters of your searches on these sites, or you may spend a substantial amount of time drifting in cyberspace! Failing that, try a search engine, and be prepared for a long trawl through the net.

Computer Assisted Theology
http://info.ox.ac.uk/ctitext/theology/

Facets of Religion - WWW Virtual Library
http://www.bcca.org/~cvoogt/Religion/

Philosophy of Religion
www.baylor.edu/~Scott_Moore/Phi_Rel_info.html#BIB

Psychology of Religion
www.psychwww.com/psyrelig/index.htm

Religious Studies

Religious Studies Web Guide
www.acs.ucalgary.ca/~lipton/format.html

Religious Tolerance
www.religioustolerance.org/

Anthropology and Religion
www.as.ua.edu/ant/Faculty/murphy/419/419www.htm
www.uwgb.edu/sar/links.htm

Sociology of Religion
Sociological Tour through Cyberspace
www.trinity.edu/~mkearl/

Voice of the Shuttle
http://vos.ucsb.edu/shuttle/religion.html

Wilfred Laurier University
www.wlu.ca/~wwwrandc/internet_links.html

further reading

The following titles will be useful if you want to read in greater depth about the religions discussed in this Guide.

David V Barrett, The New Believers: Sects, 'Cults' and Alternative Religions, (Cassell, 2nd Edition, 2001).

Henry Chadwick & GR Evans, Atlas of the Christian Church, (Macmillan, 1987).

Dan & Lavinia Cohn-Sherbok, Judaism: A Short Introduction, (Oneworld, 1999).

Damien Keown, Buddhism: A Very Short Introduction (Oxford University Press, 2000).

Owen Cole & Peggy Morgan, Six Religions in the Twenty First Century (Nelson Thornes, 2nd Edition, 2000).

Gavin Flood, An Introduction to Hinduism (Cambridge University Press, 1996).

John R. Hinnells, The New Penguin Handbook of Living Religions (Penguin Books, 2000).

Ian S Markham (editor), A World Religions Reader (Blackwell Publishers, 2nd Edition, 1999).

WH McLeod, Sikhism (Penguin, 1998).

Neal Robinson, Islam: A Concise Introduction (Curzon Press, 1999).

Ninian Smart, The World's Religions (Cambridge University Press, 2nd Edition, 1998).

Xinzhong Yao, An Introduction to Confucianism (Cambridge University Press, 2000).

Index

The Good Web Guide

www.thegoodwebguide.co.uk

The Good Web Guide provides simple one-click access to all the sites mentioned in this book, and is an easy way to start exploring the internet. All books about the internet become slightly out of date as soon they're printed, but with the free updates you'll receive as a subscriber to the Good Web Guide website, this book will remain current as long as you're a member.

The goodwebguide.co.uk homepage provides links to each of the GWG subject channels, including World Religions. It also lists headlines and links to some of the newest articles, reviews and competitions on the site, and details of special offers on other Good Web Guide books.

Although some reviews and articles are free to view, the majority of the content on the Good Web Guide site is accessible only to members. Begin by clicking on the small 'Register Now' icon near the top left of the page. When you've filled in and submitted your details a menu will appear on the left of the page. Choose the option Register a Purchase. A list of questions will appear, but you only need to answer the one relevant to this book, and you will need to have the book in front of you to find the answer. Once you're registered you'll be able to view the contents of this book online, and be eligible for free updates. As a member you can upgrade to obtain access to all the channels at a specially discounted rate.

Reviews are organised by chapter, with the new reviews in the Latest Additions section. At the bottom of each review there is a link straight to the site, so you don't have to worry about typing in the addresses. New reviews are added at

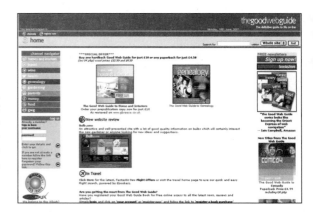

least monthly, sometimes weekly. You can also sign up for monthly free newsletters to have website reviews delivered straight to your desk.